RESTLESS

Memoir of an Incurable Traveller

Heather Hackett

First Edition 2016

ISBN: 978-0-6480093-0-6

14 13 12 11 10 / 10 9 8 7 6 5 4 3 2 1

Acknowledgements

So many people have helped me bring this book to life. And I thank you all from the bottom of my heart. Your tireless assistance, support, and unending patience have meant so much.

Without the love and support of my partner, Iain, this book could never have happened. Likewise, the encouragement of my daughter, Noa, who begged me to 'get this written, please', and my son, Mani, who lived through so many of these adventures with me. You are all so special to me. And special thanks to my Mum, who saved all the letters I wrote during our travels. You helped to keep all these memories alive.

No book is ever written in a vacuum, or complete without an editor, or several. A mighty thank you must go to Sheryl Washburn, my kick-ass, number one editor who kept asking for more; Gabby, whose comments helped more than she realised; and David, thank you for being such a stickler for detail.

Jon Collins, the brilliant photographer and eloquent writer who agreed to write my Foreword. You are a superstar.

I am supremely grateful to everyone on my launch team, a group of spectacular people who gave up their time to get behind this project, and everyone at Self-Publishing School - you guys rock.

And finally, James, who made these memories with me. None of these stories would ever have happened without you.

Thank you all.

For My Dad

Who always wanted to know

what I knew

Foreword

Our immersion with the world is never how we imagine it. We see images in magazines and watch endless documentaries or television series that depict the life of a traveller, without realising that this status comes with so much more behind it. While on the road, we are confronted with the perfections and imperfections of different corners of the planet, where situations are beyond our control, things can go wrong, and where travel is as exhausting as it is fulfilling. The true reality of being a traveller is that life often leads us in directions we never expect, to places we would never imagine going, people we wouldn't meet otherwise, and eventually, leading lives unparalleled to the ones that we left behind. Restless is the story of a traveller that discovers this reality and many more when leaving her life in Australia behind.

Growing up in a world of immense opportunity, Heather is a free-spirit and dreamer trapped in a life of expectation. Her choice to go against the grain and leave everything behind in the 80's, an era where most were told to secure a job, work hard and climb the corporate ladder, attests to her adventurous spirit and the need to know more. What better place to begin her immersion than the diverse and crowded melting pot of cultures in Asia. Heather plunges towards the heart of Asia and becomes immediately embedded into the fabric of a Thai family, sharing their single-roomed home rather than the beach and backpacker scene she'd always dreamed of in Thailand. So begins a series of captivating and humorous stories about the 'unexpected' when living almost more than a decade out of a backpack. From the havoc and beautiful chaos of India, through the tight bureaucracy and black markets of Burma, to the marvels of a European summer, or the sheer determination of shifting their lives to Japan with a nine-month-old baby and not a single grasp on the language; there is absolutely no challenge she won't accept. Heather's intimate descriptions of each of these places, the people she interacts with and the various triumphs and tribulations evokes a sense of what it feels like to be in that exact moment. Frustration. Elation. Satisfaction. Enlightenment.

Having grown up with and travelled with Heather's daughter, Noa, it is apparent her legacy and stories have transcended through time. Heather's philosophy to immerse oneself at the core of other places, cultures, languages and lives is one I've grown to see in Noa as well; in that she dreams bigger than anyone I know. As an avid traveller and curious spirit myself, I take incredible inspiration from the words in this book. Heather captures our world as a sliver of time that we will never see again; one before the modern technological conveniences of Google Maps, Translators, Airbnb and Skyscanner, which have saved me on numerous occasions.

I know that Heather's memoir will become an inspiration to others who have longed for their own immersion, or are simply reminiscent of their own journeys or experiences that have passed and ultimately changed them for better. In this sense, *Restless* is not simply about travel, as it is a memoir that touches on every element of the human spirit; adventure and fear, the rollercoaster of intimate relationships, the joy of creating life and the constant questioning of what is expected of us and what is truly possible when we put our minds and our hearts into something we love.

Jonathon Collins

Photographer

'Only the ideas we live have any value.'

From *Demian* (1919) by Herman Hesse

FREE PHOTOBOOK

Just to say thanks for purchasing my book

I'd like to give you a copy of the companion eBook containing all the photos of the journeys described in

RESTLESS

ABSOLUTELY 100% FREE!

Just go to

www.heatherjhackett.com/restless-free-photo-book/

BECOMING RESTLESS

I was born restless.

Since my early childhood I have had trouble settling. Nothing ever satisfied me. Not really. I was given so many opportunities, things that other kids would have cut off their right arm for – like ballet lessons, elocution lessons, piano lessons, even violin lessons. I played tennis, basketball, learned to water ski, sail, ten pin bowl, and spent school vacations on the beach, on Norfolk Island, and even Fiji. At Christmas time, our lounge room was awash with presents, even if our dog did destroy some of them while we were at the Christmas morning church service. I had so many options. I wanted for nothing.

Except a *Tearie Dearie* doll.

My Dad used to save up his coins in a tin he kept in his lowboy, and when the tin was full, he would tell my brother and I to fetch our money boxes. As we sat at his feet, he shared out the coins, one for one. We weren't allowed to spend the money, though. We had to put it in the bank.

My brother and I had worked out that we could get the coins out of the kangaroo-shaped boxes by inserting a knife into the slot. The coins would line up with the blade and easily fall out. We only ever had about five dollars in one-, two-, five- and ten-cent pieces. But five dollars was more than enough to buy a *Tearie Dearie* doll. They were the latest fad when I was about eight years old. They cried real tears.

And I wanted one.

I remember emptying the money box, counting the spoils, and proudly announcing to my Mum that I had enough to buy one. The answer was no. I was crushed. I pleaded. I asked why not. Apparently, I 'had enough toys.' And it was probably true. But right at that moment, that doll was the only thing in the whole world I wanted and wasn't allowed to have. I couldn't understand it. Forget *Tearie Dearie. I* cried real tears.

It was a hard lesson, but it went largely unnoticed. Sadly, it was the start of a pattern that continued throughout my teenage years. It seemed that whenever I *really* wanted something, I was denied. It might sound like I was spoilt, and there's probably some truth in that. But the things that came easy, I didn't want. And the things that mattered, I couldn't get.

And not least of these seemed to be the love and affection of my Mum. But it didn't stop me from trying endlessly to please her.

I was good at school work without much effort. I was good at most things without much effort. Things came easy to me. Too easy. You might say I was too clever for my own good. And that was a bad thing, because the one thing I hadn't learnt growing up was discipline. When the going got tough, I didn't know how to put in the effort required. And eventually, I failed. Failed to make good choices. There were too many choices, too many options. So, I buried my head in the sand and took the easy way out. I did what I was supposed to do. But I wasn't happy about it.

When I first read Hesse's *Demian*, in my final year of high school, it had a profound effect on me. I wrote all over it, and copied huge, inspiring chunks of text into my journal. I was intrigued by the idea that to really explore the world, we had to destroy the one we knew, like a chicken breaking out of its shell to be born and to grow.

Though I never set out to destroy the world I knew, in a way, that's exactly what I did.

University opened many doors for me. I could have had my pick of any number of careers. Pretty much anything except medicine or vet science. But that didn't matter because I wasn't interested in those subjects. The one door that opened that really mattered was the front door of my childhood home. I was only 17, but I had been waiting for so long.

But even once I had entered the hallowed halls, I still couldn't settle down to study. I had my first taste of freedom. And I liked it. I had had to fight with my course advisors over the subjects I was going to take. And I had lost. Clearly, a teachers' scholarship had been the wrong choice. But so was everything else I tried. Science. Optometry. Nothing was right. I failed my first year. And my third. Mum and Dad blamed James. I thanked God for him. But in the end, that relationship failed, too. We all grew apart.

Even as I was on the brink of dropping out of university, I still wanted someone to tell me I was doing the right thing. And when I looked for support from my Mum, she 'wasn't in the mood.' Her own words. They cut like a knife.

It was such a harsh awakening that, for the first time in my life, I realised I actually didn't need her approval. So, I stopped asking for it. I suppose she did me a favour. I made the decision by myself, for myself. I tore up the world I knew. And a funny thing happened - nothing. I didn't die. The world didn't end. My friends still loved me. I still had a life. I even got a job that paid real money. And Mum eventually got over it.

But because it felt so good, I kept on doing it.

When it came to travelling, the only thing I knew was that I had to do it. I devoured any books I could find that told the tales I wanted to live for myself. I even hung out at the airport at times, just to fool myself into thinking, for some short time, that I was on my way. I envied the comers and goers, imagining exotic stories with them as the lead characters. And I waited impatiently for my turn, which couldn't come quickly enough.

The day my four friends, including James, took off for Bali and the Asia overland trail without me, I was getting engaged. If ever there was a time to say, 'It should have been me,' that was it. I should have been on that plane with them. I should have been on that path. Instead, I was headed for a life of suburban normality, a life of doing what was expected of me. With the wrong man. We all knew it. But it took an act of enormous courage to change direction. And it came close to going horribly wrong.

My Mum came down to Sydney to help me organise the wedding and pick out a dress. On the way home from a day of shopping in the city, she made a comment that struck me dumb because it came right out of left field.

'I don't think you should have any children for at least five years.'

'Why not?' I asked her.

'Well, you don't seem to have very much in common.'

Those two lines, delivered so matter-of-factly, changed my life. I realised she was right. And for the first time in a long time, I listened to her. Obviously, she had implied that she thought this marriage would end in divorce. I didn't want that. In my mind, marriage was for life, and I only intended to do it once in mine. Ironically, when I took time out to consider what I really wanted, and came to the conclusion that it was the wrong way to go, she was pissed off.

'Just marry him,' she advised. 'You can always get divorced.' I sorted it out in my own mind, but for the life of me, I couldn't fathom hers.

I called off the engagement two months later. I left my mindless job and went back to college to study a course I was actually interested in – natural medicine. When James returned to Australia twelve months later, we got back together, and laid the foundations for the stories in this book. We are not together any more, and it's not my intention to discuss those issues here. Suffice to say, we share the memories on the pages that follow, and two beautiful children, whom we both love and adore.

What we have done may not necessarily be unique; it might even be quite a common thing to do these days. But back when we took off to travel, work and see the world with two very young children in tow, it was considered abnormal, irresponsible and downright dangerous. But James and I paid no mind to the naysayers, or their doom and gloom predictions for our fate. In fact, they had the opposite effect. Tell me that I can't do something and I will do it twice just to prove a point. I'm stubborn like that.

Back in the 80s, we didn't have the luxury of smart phones or the Internet, AirBnb or Trip Advisor. We had printed books, and wrote letters home by hand. And I thank my Mum for saving every single one I wrote, without which this book may never have been written.

The ideas we lived have been immensely fulfilling, but not without costs. While my friends were all graduating and becoming respectable, professional, career-oriented success stories, I was clambering up and down the Himalaya with a baby on my back, riding a bike across Europe, and living and working in Japan.

Whichever way you look at it though, my choices have made me who I am, and I wouldn't trade them or the experiences they've brought me for all the world.

Obviously, along the way I've encountered many incredible people; people with stories just like the ones that follow. In our long, late night discussions about 'the road', I'm sure they never expected to end up on the pages of a book. So, to protect their privacy, I have changed their names and sometimes their circumstances.

It is my hope that my words and thoughts will inspire you to examine your own choices, and find value in new ideas, ideas you can actually live, the way that those who went before inspired me. If so, my job is done.

Welcome to my restless world.

AND SO IT BEGAN

For years, I had heard the legend of the overland route through Asia; fantastic tales of places with exotic names where people lived different lives to mine. I had listened in awe as those who had been wove their weird and wonderful tales. They introduced me to strange Middle Eastern foods while we sat on the floors of rooms furnished only with cushions and low tables, and lit by candles.

I was so in love with the whole idea of travelling the world, that one of my most-treasured possessions was a dog-eared and marked-up copy of the Overland Bible, or *Lonely Planet's South-East Asia on a Shoestring* as they called it back then. It had been handed down from my mentors; they knew where to go because they had been there. And I had read *The Surprising Asians* and *People of Shiva*, by Frances Letters, many times over. Every name on every page inspired and intrigued. Asia, and particularly Nepal, became a dream. An Avalon. My Avalon.

There was an ad on television in the late 1970s, an ad for Amco® jeans. 'Every Amco® tells a story...' It featured many young travellers, backpackers, trekking across Asia, Europe, the world. It aired every afternoon just as I arrived home from a mind-numbing job as a public service clerk. I hurried to get home in time to see it. It had a catchy tune: *'Seen 'em three miles high, on the road to Kathmandu...'* then some young hunk threw his pack on the back of a truck and climbed in behind it. I wanted to be there, to do that.

And so it was inevitable that one day I did.

My turn came around in 1983. Six months previously, I had married James. Our wedding gifts had included backpacks, sleeping bags and other items that would be useful on the overland route through Asia. Our friends understood, but our parents didn't get it. Or approve. With all the blind naivety of youth, we didn't listen. As far as we were concerned, we were born to leave. Again, and again.

In a manner that would become typical of our travels, we didn't make any plans beyond packing our bags and buying one-way plane tickets to Singapore. Let the road rise up to meet us. After that, it all relied on serendipity.

Yet despite my voracious appetite for all things Eastern or Asian, or anything even remotely related to either, I was unprepared for my first trip out of Australia. Climatic extremes assaulted my body and a glut of spiritual alternatives set my mind ablaze. I had gone in search of answers, but a year in South East Asia only aroused more questions. I was still searching for answers.

I'm not sure what I expected to find, but I was blown away, never to see things the same way again. I have always thought of it as the true beginning of my journey.

And though it may have relied on serendipity, it wasn't all beer and skittles.

PART 1

JUST
TWO OF US

ONE

Family Thais

FROM THE DAY I STEPPED OFF THE PLANE into the heat and humidity that was Singapore, I was chasing that old dream. I was longing for the famous beaches and backpacker lifestyle that Thailand had to offer. So many travellers had made the detour across the Gulf of Siam to the string of tiny island paradises, that they had become a major pit stop on the overland route - places to relax and recuperate from the daily hassles of life on the Asian highways. Perhaps it was a bit previous of me to hanker after the easy life. After all, between Singapore, Penang and Koh Samui, life could hardly have been described as a hassle. I was still green, still learning the ways of the road. Selfishly, I just wanted to live the dream.

We had hardly done more than hit the shores of Koh Samui when we ran into Yai. He and James had become fast friends when James had visited Thailand a couple of years before. James had been one of that group of friends that had left me to deal with the engagement I mentioned earlier. Yai insisted that we stay with him, his wife, Noi, and their 3-year-old daughter. He wouldn't take no for an answer, despite my heavy protestations. I had my heart set on a lazy beach holiday. The bustling port village on Koh Samui was no match for the beaches on the east coast of the island. You can imagine my disappointment, then, when we ended up not in a thatched bungalow metres from the shore of a sparkling blue sea, but instead, housed in a wooden shed roughly the size of a small living room back home.

Their 'house' was just a room; four wooden walls, a concrete floor and a tin roof that, during the day, turned the structure into an oven. The concrete heated up to the point where sitting quickly became extremely uncomfortable. It was attached to the side of another larger house that doubled as a small shop. It was situated on the main road heading out of town toward the beaches, where I would rather have been spending my days.

But the closest I got to that dream was watching the pickups pass by full of *falang* (tourists - singular and plural, male and female) heading for the party venues, while I showered at the well in the front yard. Yes, that's right. We showered in the front yard. We drew buckets of water from the well and completed our ablutions by throwing them over our heads while wrapped in a sarong. Getting the soap off wasn't too hard, but getting shampoo out of my long hair was time-consuming. It took buckets and buckets. Maintaining decorum while keeping the sarong firmly in place was an acquired art. I wasn't very good at it. I bathed with my back to the main road, so I didn't have to face the passing parade. Or suffer any embarrassing wardrobe malfunctions.

Yai and Noi left around 9 a.m. each morning, covered from head to toe to keep the sun off. I often wondered how they survived the heat as they trudged up and down the sand, dressed as they were. But they hated what we yearned for - darker skin. They headed out to the beaches on their motorbike. Yai sold gemstones and Noi sold sarongs and T-shirts to *falang* lazing around in the sun. Some days, Yai returned in the afternoon with $500 USD in travellers' checks and cash from successful sales. None of the gems were real, but he knew all the tests, and tricks, that 'proved' they were authentic. Who falls for that?

Yai was an excellent salesman - cute and charming. Plus, his English was well beyond average. After a good day on the beach, we'd have a slap-up dinner. Yai would buy a live chicken, and kill it in the backyard. I couldn't watch either the butchering or the plucking. But hypocritically, I was quite happy to help prepare the dishes and eat the spoils.

Noi cooked everything in her one-pot kitchen, which occupied a space in the corner of the house. Her stove consisted of a single concrete bucket with openings cut into the bottom to make room for a small fire of coconut husks. The top was fitted with extensions that were just right to hold a large saucepan of rice, or a wok. The rice was always cooked first, a practice we learnt and put to good use on our own single gas burner stove when we were camping our way around Europe. She never failed to whip up a feast while squatting beside her stove/bucket.

I learnt a lot from the simple lives our friends lived. I saw them living with so much less than we, as westerners, were used to. I couldn't even begin to imagine how to prepare a meal for four people using a bucket, one saucepan and a wok. More than likely, I would have been outraged if asked to do so. I can hear myself saying words to the effect of, 'Bugger off! Let's just get take out.' Anyone who knew me would have known better than to ask. And the only discussion would have been over which menu to choose from. Seeing how hard they worked to earn a living and to provide for their family, I felt guilty. Guilty for being so soft. And for longing to be at the beach, lazing in the sun.

Noi also taught me how to make a bed out of a mattress on the floor that needed to be packed away each morning to make room for life. Any flat sheet could easily be turned into a fitted one by tying knots in each corner and stretching the cloth across all four corners of the mattress. A top sheet was unnecessary in the heat and humidity. Several well-placed mosquito coils, on the other hand, were mandatory. With the sheets tied in this fashion, each morning the mattress could simply stand on its end in one of the unused corners of the room, still made up and ready to go again in the evening. So practical.

Noi's wardrobes consisted of ropes strung between the struts of the unclad, wooden walls of the room. Embarrassingly, I had more variety in my backpack than they had in the whole house. The contents of these makeshift cupboards changed regularly, as sometimes they would swap their wares for other items of coveted Western-style clothing - especially brand name jeans and t-shirts.

Yai and Noi thought of us as family; I think they did from the start. It was just us that had to get our heads around it. We certainly weren't used to sharing a living space so closely with others. Or a child. But here, it was just life. They shared a lot of things we thought of as private property or personal issues. The line between 'mine' and 'yours' was very blurry. As we began to be integrated into their extended family, we were constantly asked for money - five baht, ten baht, fifty baht, even five hundred baht on several occasions. Of course, it was only right that we should contribute to the costs of meals and family outings, and we gladly did so. At first, I felt annoyed that we were being used as a source of cash, simply because we were foreigners. Or so I thought. But I soon came to realise that it was another part of the Thai definition of family, and that other siblings and cousins were also asked to share the expenses. It was really a small price to pay for the window on life in Thailand that we had been given. And wasn't that the reason I had wanted to travel in the first place? To see another side of life?

We were invited to meet Mama and Papa, who were visiting from their village just outside the city of Ayutthaya, north of Bangkok. As respected family elders, they were treated like visiting royalty. They were quite old, but looked much older than they really were. Life may have been simple, but it was obviously tough. For some reason, Papa took quite a shine to me. He told everyone I was a 'good girl'.

Whenever we visited, which we were obliged to do each afternoon, he insisted that I sit next to him on the floor and share some food and conversation. He would talk away to me in Thai as if I understood every word he said. But I spoke only a few words of the language, and he spoke not a word of English. The parts of the language I could understand led me to believe that all they talked about was money, since I heard the words *ha baht* (five baht) mentioned with monotonous regularity in every conversation. I sat politely, listened and smiled, and everyone was happy.

The day before they left to return home, we were invited to attend lunch. Mama and her daughters had prepared a feast which included salmon steaks, and chicken and buffalo curries of all colours. When the family killed and cooked a chicken, nothing was wasted. The parts of the bird that couldn't be used in the curries were made into chicken soup. This ended up being mostly giblets and bones. Unfortunately, I was seated next to Papa at the luncheon, and the appetiser was giblet soup.

Papa himself had filled a bowl for me that was absolutely swimming in all the 'good' bits. The first spoonful I put in my mouth contained something unmentionable and I could neither bring myself to chew it nor swallow it whole. Spitting it out was not an option. It didn't take long before the gag reflex kicked in and I sat there desperately trying to keep my mouth closed and the abominable contents inside my cheeks. Papa was oblivious to my plight and chatted on relentlessly, reminding me several times how *aloi mak mak* (really delicious) the soup was. That was another term I understood well, but on this occasion, not one with which I could concur. In fact, I couldn't even open my mouth to agree, lest the piece of stomach or eyeball fell out. I nodded and smiled as best I could with a mouthful of chicken giblets.

I must have sat like that for a good ten minutes, pretending to indulge in more of the soup. Finally, a break in conversation allowed me to excuse myself on the pretence of needing the bathroom. It wasn't far from the truth, and I rushed outside to spit in the garden. I think I brought up everything I'd eaten over the last week, such was my disgust for the contents of my mouth. When I went back inside, I complimented the chefs, Mama and all the female siblings, and quickly filled my plate with other things. Somehow, the whole debacle went unnoticed.

Another endearing habit of the family, when they shared a meal, was to very literally share the meal. To make sure that I got enough to eat, and sampled every dish, they would put more food on my plate whenever I got close to finishing. This was all well and good when I was enjoying the meal. If I happened to dislike any of it, or had eaten so much I couldn't fit in even one more mouthful, I was screwed. Sadly, I wasn't a big fan of rice back then. Or fish, one of their staples. After each mouthful, I drank copious amounts of water to wash it down. That was a big mistake. The rice swelled in my stomach, and I was full to bursting after eating very little. As a result, I lost lots of weight in Thailand.

The Thais have a tradition of giving each other nicknames, often relating to what they look like. Since our arrival, I had been called *Uon*. When I asked what it meant, they said, 'Little bit fat.' I wasn't impressed. And it hadn't made me feel any happier to be spending my days lounging around in a sweat shed instead of a hammock. But with the weight loss came an unexpected boost in confidence and self-esteem. I began to care less about the nickname the family had given me, because it started to be untrue. Since high school, I had been on one starvation diet or another for most of my life. And they had never worked for me. Here, the weight just seemed to drop off without much effort. It was another dream come true, and I was elated.

My rapid weight loss, and the uplift in self-esteem that accompanied it, brought with it another issue that I hadn't bargained on. I didn't notice it at first; I was too busy feeling good about my new image. I'd never thought of myself as attractive, and it was surprising to me that

I had become 'noticeable'. Yai's attentions were subtle, and at first I thought I might have been imagining things that weren't there. But when I looked more closely, I was thrilled and excited by the sexual tension we were creating.

I couldn't tell James, and he hadn't noticed what was going on. He and Yai had grown close, and spent many hours together visiting Yai's friends who lived up in the hills behind town. James even went selling on the beach with Yai on several occasions; it was like the final tourist authentication of the fake gems that helped them sell. I spent those times getting to know Noi, who confided to me that she was worried about where they had gone, and what they were up to. For some reason, she didn't like Yai's friends.

We spent our days in the village frequenting the shops and restaurants near the pier and watching the constant influx and efflux of tourists on the lunchtime ferry. It made its way from the mainland city of Suratthani to Koh Phangan via Nathon each day, depositing yet another load of tourists bound for the beaches. They were a motley crew, searching for some respite from the rigours of the road, and hungry for some fun and excitement. The locals were only too happy to oblige, feeding them the food they were used to and the lifestyle they yearned for in exchange for their hard-earned dollars. It was a fair swap. And when they had had their fill, they loaded themselves back onto the pickups and boats and headed back to the mainland to find the next stop on the overland adventure.

I couldn't help thinking it had become a treadmill. I know not all of us were escaping the mindless, daily routine of nine-to-five jobs, but had we just traded one form of insanity for another? Sure, this new reality was of our own design, at our own leisure. But was it better? Were we learning? Did we even want to learn anything?

Although I had arrived in Thailand longing for the beach and 'the scene', I came to believe we were better off with the family. Whether I was wrong or right may have been a moot point, but this experience was different; no more or less valid, and probably not unique, but different. Most likely it shaped our future more than we realised at the time. James and I became un-tourists, travellers who created their stories based more on what they hadn't seen and done rather than what they had. We shared the same paths, but not the same companions. In Thailand, at least, we were more like voyeurs, trapped between two worlds, watching both, but belonging to neither.

TWO

A Beach Called Haadrin

AFTER ALMOST A MONTH WITH OUR THAI FAMILY, we all needed a break - us from them and them from us. One small square of concrete between four people and a toddler had become far too crowded. Yai and Noi sent us forth on the ferry to Koh Phangan with a little square of paper containing the name of a long lost relative, Mr Kao, written in Thai. He owned a set of bungalows on a beach called Haadrin on the east coast of the island. It was only a short, 40-minute trip across the water to the outer island, on a boat that closely resembled the fuselage of a defunct aeroplane, and about as suited to water transport.

When we arrived at the port, it was almost dead low tide, and the boat could not get close enough to the pier for us to disembark. We were offloaded into a flotilla of long tail boats that flitted back and forth to the shore, emptying passengers and cargo alike. There were only a handful of foreigners on the boat with us, and only two of those had even heard of Haadrin. As often happens on the road, the four of us united for mutual support. The others were herded into waiting taxis-cum-pickups and taken off to resorts on the west coast, quite near to the port village of Tongsala.

We offered our note to a well-dressed man who asked us if we needed a bungalow. He wasn't the long lost relative we were seeking, but he seemed nice, and he had his own bungalows on Haadrin. He promised to help us find our friend, and we believed him. He introduced himself as Mr Chan.

The remoteness of the island and relatively small population meant that there weren't many actual roads. Mr Chan guided us towards a tribe of waiting motorcyclists. It took four bikes to accommodate us, including our two new companions and our back packs. It wasn't long before the dirt road petered out and we were winding our way along narrow trails amid thick coconut palms, hanging on to our guides for grim death as we bounced up and down and side to side. Every now and then I was slapped in the face by an errant palm frond crossing our path.

The southern coastline of Koh Phangan was fringed by a coral reef, exposed at low tide. We arrived at a small communal building on the edge of what would have been the water had it not been for the low tide. Looking out across the mud flat that had replaced the water, we hoped that this was not our final destination, though there didn't appear to be any form of accessible transport going anywhere else.

Our motorbike guides advised us in broken English that we needed to take a boat to Haadrin, but for the life of us we couldn't see one anywhere. On further questioning, they pointed to a tiny speck of a canoe, beached on the mud flats about 100 metres from the shore. Excellent. Not.

We waited about 40 minutes for Mr Chan to appear. He seemed to know everyone, and went off in search of the owner of the boat. On his return, with another four young men in tow, we began the trek out to the boat. It was almost impossible, wading through ankle-deep water in flip flops, teetering this way and that, trying to keep ourselves and our packs dry at all costs. But we needn't have bothered.

Once we reached the tiny boat, to our dismay, it was full of water. Our guides began furiously bailing it out. This didn't bode well for the journey ahead, considering there were now nine of us and four backpacks to squeeze aboard. We realised now why we had had to wait so long for the captain to appear. There was no point in him arriving earlier because there was not enough water to float the boat and get it back over the coral reef into open water. The prospect of going into open water in such a vessel was disturbing, to say the least.

Somehow, Mr Chan and the two young guides manhandled the decrepit hull across the rest of the shallow bay to the reef, where we were all instructed to get in. And start bailing. It seemed like a desperate enterprise, since with all the occupants and our luggage, the boat barely floated anyway. Our survival seemed to be at risk, so we all obeyed.

We putt-putted down the coast just outside the reef for about half an hour. At a seemingly random point, it was decided that we probably weren't going to make it back across the reef before dark. This time, it was us who had to bail out, and we all stepped out onto the reef in chest-deep water. We staggered ashore, holding our bum bags above our heads, leaving the four Thai men to battle with the luggage, the waves, and the incoming tide.

We waited on the shore in the gathering darkness with our new friends, a Canadian couple from Alberta. One of them produced a spliff and passed it around. None of us spoke much after that. We just sat there, staring at the distant lights of Koh Samui with big, goofy grins on our faces. There was nothing to say. We stopped caring whether they even managed to save our luggage. It was just beautiful, and so quiet.

Eventually, the situation on the reef was deemed hopeless and another man went out in yet another boat to rescue our luggage. The entire exercise had taken more than two hours, and it was now completely dark.

Reunited with our packs, we set off down a jungle track in single file, following Mr Chan, who had the only torch. It wasn't easy. The light was dim and the path uneven. We thought it was hilarious. Mr Chan quickly worked out why, and laughed along with us. After about 15 minutes, we emerged from the jungle onto a beach. There was a cool breeze blowing in over the water, bringing the fresh salt smell of the sea to us. Only starlight lit the beach, and in the distance, the little bamboo lamps of Mr Chan's restaurant bobbed and swayed as if dancing in the night air.

At the other end of the beach, we could see an array of fluorescents. Nothing bobbed or swayed down there. Mr Chan pointed out that that was Mr Kao's bungalows and offered to lead the way there. But it just didn't appeal. I'd always hated fluorescent lighting. We opted for the magic of the dancing lights and sand-floor restaurant instead.

By day, the pristine white sand beach was warm, quiet and relaxing, everything you'd expect from a tropical paradise. It was heaven come to earth, hauntingly beautiful, and a welcome respite from the flurry and din of Koh Samui. We stayed over two weeks, relaxing in the lap of simple luxury. Mr Chan had a ready supply of what he liked to call 'flower'. It was potent weed, and we inhaled deeply. Mrs Chan was an excellent cook and managed to keep up with our heightened sense of hunger. The days melted into one another. Neither James nor I wanted to ever leave. I'd found my beach scene. It was better than I had dreamed, and I had dreamed big. I wasn't going to give it up in a hurry. But eventually, and with deep sadness, I did.

My reluctance to leave Haadrin stemmed from a strong connection to what I could only describe as its energy. Unsullied by human interaction, it had remained pure and unspoiled, raw and wild. There were no footprints in the sand. With each high tide, all traces of us were washed away. Every day and every night, nature conspired to return the beach to a normal that didn't contain our presence. If we had never come this way, nothing would have changed. It would have continued just as it was, just as it had always been. But because I had seen it, I couldn't help but be overcome with awe and respect. I wanted to protect it, to have it remain the same forever. But three

years later, when I returned, I would learn the hard way that this
could never be, except in my memory. Progress follows us, and often
overtakes us. And we lose control of that we seek to protect.

The return trip to Koh Samui meant an early morning departure from
Haadrin. The ferry didn't leave the dock until around 11 a.m., but we
had a walk, a boat-ride, and a motorbike trip through the jungle to
navigate. Mr Chan, always smiling, accompanied us the entire way. I
think maybe he liked the odd bit of 'flower' himself. He would do his
shopping for the restaurant and wait in town for the next ferry to
arrive. Since hardly anyone had heard of Haadrin, he had to work
hard to attract his clientele. But the sheer beauty of the beach ensured
that this was not going to be the case forever. Having witnessed the
full moon from the Haadrin sands, I knew it wouldn't take long. And
I knew I would be back one day. I just didn't bargain on everyone else
on earth finding out about it in the meantime.

Life quickly returned to normal back in Nathon with the family. We
tried to convince Yai and Noi to go back to Haadrin with us, so that
we could share some of the beauty we had discovered with them. But
fiscal concerns won out, and the lack of *falang* lazing on the beach was
not a draw card for them, as it was for us. They didn't care for a
holiday. A holiday meant no income for them. It was another way we,
as westerners, were fundamentally different from our new friends.

As the summer months turned wetter, because it never really got
cooler near the equator, and the tourist numbers started to diminish,
Yai and Noi found it more and more difficult to sell their goods on the
beaches. As was their practice, they would retreat north to Ayutthaya
for the monsoon. As part of the family, they expected that we would
accompany them. So we did.

THREE

Living in Ayutthaya

THE TRIP FROM THE ISLAND TO THE COUNTRYSIDE north of Bangkok was long and arduous, and punctuated with rice paddies. And the music of *Icehouse*, a soundtrack that became synonymous with my experience of Thailand. To this day, I can't hear the deep, throbbing base intro to *Great Southern Land* or *Street Cafe* without it pulling on my heart strings. So many miles covered on Thai trains, headphones firmly connected to the Walkman, reminiscing about the life I'd left and how different it was to the life I was living. I'd travelled across the seas in search of something else. Yet it was the friends I'd left behind that I missed the most. And those songs, from a past becoming ever more distant, dragged me back, kept me connected to a time that would never be again.

We had taken the slow, overnight train from Suratthani with the family, about eight of them when all the extended hangers-on were counted up. And we had spent most of the trip sleeping on the carriage floor between seats or in the aisles. It was more comfortable than the hard seats of third class. Our fellow passengers were all doing the same thing, which made every trip to the bathroom especially problematic. But by midnight, most of the seats had been abandoned, left to old ladies and babies.

The family in Ayutthaya all lived in one enormous wooden house, weathered grey with age. It was large and open and airy, with hardly a stick of furniture, apart from a few cupboards and a single small TV. The only decorations on the walls were photographs of the beloved King and Queen, and religious images and texts from the Qur'an.

By day, the main communal room was empty. By night, it transformed into a tent city, as each of the siblings erected a mosquito net over a double mattress to house their family. There were 14 brothers and sisters in all, ranging in ages from seven to thirty-two, and the older ones were married with children of their own. As most of the family had returned home for *Ramadan*, each night I counted at least eight 'tents'.

After our initial introductions on arrival, we hardly ever saw Yoh, the patriarch of the family. He spent his entire day in his own room, reading from the Qur'an. The house stood within earshot of the local mosque, and every evening at sunset we were treated to the sound of the *mooasin* calling the faithful to prayer. At the same time, the crescent moon and star, the symbols of Islam, rose in the evening sky like magic. It was the first time I had truly understood the significance of the celestial connection.

Everyone was restless during the days of *Ramadan*. No work was done and no food consumed until evening. At sunset, however, the kitchen became a hive of activity, as all the sisters converged to prepare the evening meal and talk, talk, talk. I was invited to participate and to prepare our own dishes. Being vegetarian proved a difficult concept for the family to deal with. It was only fair that I either pitch in, or humbly accept what was offered.

Conversation was rapid and non-stop in the kitchen, though without much of the language to back me up, it was more like a baptism of fire. The fact that I knew hardly any Thai didn't stop them all from bombarding me with questions about our diet, our families, our home. When I couldn't understand, they simply turned their attention to Noi to provide a translation. I'm sure they thought us a little strange, but even so, we were welcomed as insiders to a culture we quickly came to appreciate and respect.

Down the road from where we were staying stood a massive, old Buddhist *stupa*. Every afternoon, just on sunset, we would take a walk past the primary school and climb the ancient stairs to sit quietly on the platform, high above the rice paddies. It became a time of quiet contemplation, which I often used to reflect on the life I had left at home. I searched for meaning, understanding, something that would make it easier to deal with. Our departure had forced a wedge between me and my family. Actually, my marriage to James had pretty much done that. Not everyone was happy about the union. My Dad was old school, and believed that the man should do the courting. But I was 12 months older than James. I had my drivers' licence. And we had two cars. There was always a curfew. And I always broke it. It was hard for Dad to deny me access to one of the cars, even though he always threatened it. I knew it bothered him.

Other things bothered him, too, like the rebel effect James appeared to have on me. Up until I met him, I had been Dad's little girl, a 'good girl', doing what was right, what I was supposed to do. I had never been game to do otherwise. To him, it must have looked like it was all James' fault. But it was just me becoming me, waiting for that door to open. Being the generous and patient man he was, he worried in silence.

Years later, when we decided to marry and take off to see the world, I'm sure he was disappointed. Leaving the country without a plan to return had only sealed our fate. And the relationship wouldn't recover for a good many years down the track. It saddened me. I felt misunderstood.

Yet this Thai family, so different from my own, had just accepted me. Perhaps they hadn't tried to understand me. Of course, they didn't have the same expectations or lifelong attachment to me that only the parent-child-sibling relationship could bring. I could be gone tomorrow, and maybe they could care less. But it didn't matter. Life was more transient here. People came and went, going where they needed to go, being where they needed to be, doing what they needed to do. There was a tacit understanding of why that didn't seem to require an explanation.

We, too, came and went from their home, and their lives - to Bangkok to purchase tickets to Nepal; and to Chang Mai just for the hell of it. It was Yai who wanted to go to Chang Mai. On our own we probably wouldn't have bothered. We were ready for Nepal. But at his insistence, we found ourselves aboard a train heading north towards the Golden Triangle. It wasn't until much later that I understood why. Yai had wanted this trip to Chang Mai so badly because of me. He wanted time away from his family to pursue the connection that had formed between us. And he manipulated both James and I perfectly to achieve his aim. By our separate actions, we played right into his hands.

And still James didn't see it. To me, it looked like he wasn't interested in seeing it. Because he didn't seem all that interested in me. At least, that's how I interpreted the situation. At a time in my life when I finally felt confident in myself, finally free to be me, I couldn't understand why the one person who should have been there for me, should have protected me, should have fought for me, wasn't and didn't. So, the attention from Yai was both flattering and exciting. But it was a disaster for our marriage.

When we arrived back in Ayutthaya, Noi knew immediately where we had been for over a week, and why. She made me promise not to tell James, sure that he wouldn't understand the way she did. But I told him, anyway. How could I not? But she had been right. He was upset, and reacted badly. The night before we left Thailand, he stayed in the house next door. We tried to talk, but couldn't. We cried a lot.

He told me he was flying to Kathmandu the next day, as planned. He asked me if I was going, too. I said yes; but I didn't feel very welcome.

I had hoped things might get a bit easier once we got away from Thailand, and eventually they did. But they got a lot worse first.

FOUR

The Seed and the Shoot

WE FLEW IN TO KATHMANDU IN THE LATE AFTERNOON, over a broad patchwork valley of greens and yellows. From the air, tiny brown boxes littered the ground as though they lay where they had fallen, like tumbled dice. To the north and east of the city were endless lines of snow-capped peaks. To the south, steeply-terraced hills marched ever lower toward the steaming Indian plains. My breath it simply took away.

But the dreamy arrival shattered right outside the main doors of the airport. It seemed that every young man in Kathmandu had come to the airport in taxis that looked no different to regular cars. Since they weren't allowed inside the arrival hall, hordes of them choked the exit doors, all yelling the names of different hotels and offering dirt cheap fares to get there. The catch, of course, was that you had to stay at their hotel, or the one which paid them a small commission to get you there, at least for the night. It seemed a small price to pay in the face of such competition and struggle.

A young boy with a snotty face and wrapped in dusty white linen tried to take my backpack. Before I realised it wasn't a free service, he had hauled it onto the roof of our lift and stuck out his hand for coins. I started to protest but he looked at me, just looked at me. It cost me a *rupee* – about two cents.

We didn't leave the airport immediately. The driver called to several young lads, and when there were two too many of us in the taxi, we laboured out of the car park. The road was smooth and tree-lined and curved quietly around on the outskirts of Greater Kathmandu. An incongruously, tall building appeared on the right, a five-star hotel with a casino. It looked odd, out of place, and half finished.

The road began to fill with traffic; at first more cars, then colourful trucks and overloaded buses, then people on bikes, and scooters, in rickshaws, and on foot, with water buffalo, or an elephant, and policemen with very clean, blue uniforms. And lots of cows.

It was as much the sounds and smells of the city as it was the sights, that shocked and amazed. It was an attack on all the senses, all at once. The bells of the bicycle rickshaws, the putt-putt of motorcycle rickshaw engines, truck horns, electric buses, people talking, crying babies strapped to women's backs with cloth, street *wallahs* cooking, a whole street of footpath shoeshine guys, the rot and stench of open drains, kids showering at the communal taps, old men in brilliant white wraps and jaunty caps. And stray dogs.

Then suddenly, around the next bend, an exquisite temple carved in wood, reaching gracefully for the evening sky, swathed in incense. Kathmandu seemed a study in contrast; old, new; beautiful, ugly; charming, disgusting; yang, and yin. It was overpowering.

Knowing the city from his previous visit a couple of years earlier, James wanted to stay at the same hotel, The Blue Angel. The taxi boys knew it, and after some argument about other, better places, they agreed to take us there. When we got out of the car, it was not the right place. The sign said New Blue Angel Hotel in big bold letters. James wanted the old one. I suggested we leave our bags and go look for it. Maybe we would stumble across it on our walk.

Apparently, we were in the right neighbourhood, but James needed to get his bearings, and he took off in the direction of a tall tower that dominated the horizon at the top of a narrow, gravelly lane. It was lined on either side with high brick walls that I couldn't see over. He seemed to know where he was going, but he walked so fast I struggled to keep up. The city was so strange, so dirty, so full of life. And I was lost, physically and emotionally. I almost considered stopping and watching him speed off ahead of me. It seemed as if he were trying to lose me anyway, for he never once looked back to see if I was behind him. But my survival instinct was stronger, and I hurried to catch up again.

We did an entire loop of the Kathmandu he remembered, without speaking. And we arrived back at the place where we had started - right outside The New Blue Angel. Confused, I turned to look back the way we had come; and then I saw it. Standing on the other side of the road, perched high on a hill just beyond the gravelly lane, was the old Blue Angel. For some reason, that annoyed the hell out of me. But I said nothing. I felt like I had lost the right to argue.

The hotel turned out to be a rambling, tenement building with assorted nationalities in residence along with the backpackers. It was a commanding presence in its bright blue coat of paint. We retrieved our backpacks and crossed the road to the entrance.

We were greeted enthusiastically by several young men in caps, who occupied a room just off the main entrance hall. They showed us to a similar room on the second floor with a window overlooking the front yard and street. After haggling briefly, we agreed on 30 rupees a night – about 60 cents.

But we didn't get five-star luxury for 60 cents a night. What we got was a small cold room with a cement-tiled floor, bright sky-blue walls, an unprotected bulb hanging from the ceiling for light (a very loose term), and two single wooden beds with thin mattresses, grubby pillows in green cases, and a checked sheet. The walls had a couple of wells that could be used for shelves, and the window was hung with a limp curtain that almost allowed privacy, when the light was out. The bathroom (another loose term) was down the hall, and judging from the smell emanating from it, a place to avoid for as long as humanly possible.

Electricity was a tenuous concept. It came and went at different hours of the day, and along with it, the availability of hot water for a shower. Showering required two hours' notice anyway, that being the time for it took for the heater to be turned on to warm the water. It was usually only lukewarm after two hours because someone had forgotten to turn it on when asked. There was a lag of about 30 to 40 minutes, and sometimes it required a reminder. There was never any rush involved. We nicknamed one of the reception fellows Lurch, because whenever we spoke to him, he merely wobbled his head and muttered guttural sounds reminiscent of his namesake from *The Addams Family*.

We were often forced to read and write by candlelight at night, or to walk home from dinner in pitch darkness, cautiously making our way by the light of other people's torches. Batteries were cheap but unreliable. And the streets were often running with little streamlets from the nearest communal tap.

Despite the difficult amenities, something about the Kathmandu Valley and its people pulled me in further, infected me. I fell in love with the dusty streets that often smelled of rotting refuse, the teeming hordes and the joy with which they celebrated life, the seething temples, the howling of the dogs at night, and the sounds of an Asian city coming to life in the early morning. Things that would have frustrated and annoyed me at home were suddenly things I found endearing. Why was I so willing to overlook the shortcomings of this third world city, and at the same time, rage against the same inconsistencies of my own home town? How could I reconcile these contradictions in my own personality? Why did I feel so at home here, in a place where I so obviously didn't belong?

In Kathmandu, amid the smoky, marijuana haze of the cafes and the cacophony of the streets, I had the opportunity to reflect on that very irony. I realised that, for this brief moment in my life, I was no longer being judged. Nobody knew me. Nobody knew where I was or what I was doing. Nobody even cared whether I was alive. Not really. Not here and now. I was almost alone. It offered me a sense of freedom I had never known. I had spent a lot of my life trying to live up to someone else's expectations, trying to do the 'right' thing. Hoping for validation and approval. Here, on the road, and it really wouldn't have mattered where it was, I was free of that burden. It could have happened anywhere, but it happened in Kathmandu. The 'aha moment' that redefined my life and finally set me free. For that, I will always love Nepal.

Music played a big part in my reaction to Kathmandu and Nepal. It had always been a big part of my life, strongly tied to the way I processed my interactions with the world. When I was sad, I listened to music. It helped me work things out in my head the way no words ever could. It was probably the reason I wasn't great at expressing my feelings verbally.

James and I only had a couple of cassette tapes and one Sony Walkman between us, and I dominated its use. I was the kind of person who, if I liked a song, would listen to it over and over, and at high volume. It used to drive my neighbours in my college dorm insane. The songs of Crosby, Stills, Nash and Young, though quite old even back then, spoke directly to my heart. In our dingy hotel room in Kathmandu, I listened to them endlessly, and ascribed a deeper meaning to every soulful lyric.

James and I tried to talk about what had happened in Thailand during the month we spent in Nepal. But talking about our feelings wasn't a strong point for either of us. There was a lot of silence between the words. It did get a little bit easier, and eventually, tiny windows appeared in the wall that had grown up between us. We managed to reach a tentative truce, and got on with the business of planning for India.

Kathmandu lived up to everything I had imagined. All the wild stories told by my mentors were true. Yet it stunned me by being more than I could ever have imagined, too. Maybe because of what I had been through in Thailand, or maybe in spite of it, walking the streets and drinking in the atmosphere was intoxicating. My emotions were raw and my heart was vulnerable. And Kathmandu captured me.

FIVE

Hanging Out

Kathmandu Style

THE STREETS OF KATHMANDU WERE DUSTY thoroughfares, narrow and overhung with heavily-carved windows from which washing up water regularly flew, dousing all those below. Cobbled here and there, but always shared by too many rickshaws, bicycles, people and animals, the streets teemed with the medieval grunt of life. It was one of my favourite things about Asia; people lived their normal lives in the streets with their neighbours and friends, while we in the west lived behind walls, sharing our time on our own terms, by invitation only.

I missed my friends. I missed our long, rambling conversations around the dining table that ran late into the night over too many bottles of cheap wine. I imagined what a good chat we could have if we all got together here in this unfettered atmosphere. I wondered what everyone was doing at home. Was it business as usual? Was that making them happy?

Here in Asia, it was all coffee and cake. Days ran into each other till it was difficult to tell what day it was. Except that the Kathmandu City Post Office was always closed on Friday, so that was a clue.

People came and went, and came back again. And those of us that were still here remembered them. Many travellers kept coming back to Kathmandu for respite from all the other difficult destinations within and around Nepal – the mountains, the jungles, India. It was also cheap, really cheap.

When we weren't checking our mail at the Poste Restante, we hung together in cake shops and restaurants, reading, eating, writing in our diaries, smoking hash, eating, swapping travel stories, more eating, writing letters, and planning our next moves over lots of sweet desserts. We were friends of the road, whenever our paths crossed. We sought trekking advice from those who had been. We got tips on where to stay in the western city of Pokhara, the other main Nepal destination. And the best ways into India.

There were lots of things to do and see in Nepal, and none of them cost much, financially anyway. But the emotional and physical rewards made some of them priceless. Nothing was easy, and everything was basic. It was the hard way, or the hard way. But even as the trivia of daily life unexpectedly turned into major dramas, the bigger picture became clearer, a less nebulous idea. Or that's how it seemed when we kicked back.

We looked for answers to the bigger questions, and found ourselves bogged down in details. You had to laugh at the irony of it all.

Some of the most popular places to hang out in Kathmandu were the coffee shops and restaurants of Freak Street, a narrow winding thoroughfare that was little more than a grubby alleyway, leading from Durbar Square in the centre of the city to the popular backpacker neighbourhood of Bhote Bahal. It was lined with open-fronted shops, dark, cold and musty on the inside, lit by the ubiquitous single light bulb hanging from the roof. Young lads loitered menacingly in the low doorways, accosting passers-by in hoarse whispers, 'Psst! You want hash? Brown sugar? Cocaine? Change money?' It was like running a gauntlet.

At the top of Freak Street, just off Durbar Square, was a popular bar called the Yin and Yang. It was also a hotel, but it stood out because of the huge painted black and white Tao sign on the front doors, and the throbbing music that pumped from its interior day and night. People were constantly milling in the doorway, many of whom seemed to be at the end of their roads. They were always spilling in or out of the place, a constant trickle of sordid sheiks and global riff-raff.

Then one rainy afternoon it was us in the line, nervously following our Nepali friend Ram, who couldn't believe we had never been inside, and insisted we have the experience. To be honest, the clientele had intimidated me, and I had decided to spare myself the embarrassment of entering and most likely making a fool of myself. But I really had no idea what to expect inside. And that frightened me.

We entered a darkened hallway filled with wet shoes. It was obvious we had to take ours off. The smell of marijuana smoke filled our nostrils. A heavy curtain embroidered with sequins separated the reception hall from the main bar area. As Ram pulled it aside for us to enter, it took time for my eyes to adjust to the semi darkness.

We stood in a tiered room, lit by small lights hanging strategically from the ceiling over low coffee tables. On every tier, in various stages of cushioned repose, lay a melting pot of nations and cultures, wrapped in cloths, turbans, and soft, flowing *kurtas*.

Our arrival was noted and acknowledged by an atmospheric parting of the crowd to make way for us. A table was free on the middle level, and Ram sailed gracefully over the first-tier customers to get to it. I, on the other hand, tripped and stumbled awkwardly over turbans and cappuccinos. I tried to appear nonchalant and wise, like I was a regular visitor. But inside my chest, my heart pumped furiously.

It was some time before we could catch a waiter's eye; they seemed quite dozy. Pink Floyd's *Wish You Were Here* pulsed through the room, drowning any hope of conversation. In here, communication took place on another level. It was all non-verbal and very seductive.

Someone tapped me on the shoulder from behind and asked if I had a match. I passed over the box, then watched in disbelief as it began a journey around the tables to the other side of the room. A turbaned young man with stunning black eyes and an oiled moustache dipped his head and smiled just slightly. At me!? I felt my face redden in the semi darkness, both embarrassed and flattered by the brazen ruse to get my attention.

I looked back quickly to Ram, who was taking an elaborately-rolled joint from someone at the table behind us. With all the smoke in the air, it seemed superfluous to actually smoke anything. Pink Floyd's *Time* began playing on the stereo. Soon the only thing I was completely aware of was the beat and the music.

It didn't seem to matter; everyone was occupying the same space, but living out private fantasies in their imagined experience of Kathmandu. It was a head trip in the true sense. It offered me a space to sit down and think without interruption. We stayed for hours, shamelessly inhaling the atmosphere. All those stories I'd heard as I'd sat awestruck in inner-Sydney lounge rooms, all the places I'd imagined while watching that Amco® ad so many years ago, they were all real. I was being there, doing it. And it was brilliant.

We spent a month in Kathmandu, visiting temples and shrines, riding the ring road that circled the valley, and frequenting the many bookshops. We spent hours just laying back in our hotel room, reading, talking, listening to music, and trying to repair our relationship. And mentally preparing for the challenges of India that lay directly ahead. We gleaned all we could from books and other travellers, asking endless questions about where to go, where to stay, and what to do. But at the end of the day, the only way to find out what India was like, was to go. First stop, Raxaul on the India/Nepal border.

SIX

A Punjabi Suit Please

OUR TICKETS FROM KATHMANDU to Raxaul landed us on our first bone-shaking, Nepali bus, winding up through Patan to the rim of the Kathmandu Valley, then following the river through the gorge and south west to the *terai* or plains. The further we travelled away from Kathmandu, the lower the socioeconomic status of the general population seemed. It was reflected in their houses, which changed from bricks and cement in the valley, to cobblestone, then mud and dung, and finally to thatched straw as we neared the Indian border.

The landscape also changed dramatically, from some of the world's highest peaks, to the endless, flat plains of Northern India. Not forgetting the heat and the dust.

Crossing the border in a rickshaw late one afternoon, I had a little time to reflect on the difficulties I imagined that travelling in India might bring my way: the endless road and rail trips, the heat, the hunger, the thirst, the toilets, the crowds, the beggars, the sheer headiness of it all. Would it be worth it? We hadn't even gotten there yet. I suppose I really had no idea what to expect, short of the knowledge that I had always wanted to visit this fascinating country. It scared me just enough to have spent a whole month in Kathmandu procrastinating. But it intrigued me just enough to ensure it remained on my bucket list. I had to go. No choice. But many times in the coming weeks, I had occasion to consider the saying, 'Be careful what you wish for.'

Since the Indian border town of Raxaul was just a pit stop on route to Varanasi, we needed onward tickets. This meant yet another bus ride, one leaving at 2:30 in the morning. As I sat outside the bus ticket office, studying my *Lonely Planet India* guide for a decent place to eat, I noticed a young man in a startlingly white suit standing at the edge of the road. He was obvious because of the colour of his clothes. Plus, he was staring straight at me with a weird, Mona Lisa smile. I went back to my book, hoping he would just go away.

When I looked up again, he was standing over me with a single red rose in his outstretched hands. With deep respect, he offered it to me without a word. I couldn't accept it. I said no many times. I shook my head and motioned for him to go away. He didn't. He insisted. I had no choice. Hesitantly, I took it from him. He bowed slightly, as if in awe, and left me holding the rose, retreating to the other side of the road.

How on earth would I ever explain this to James? His trust in me was still shaky. When he returned with our bus tickets, he was shocked.

'Where did you get that?' he asked. I pointed at the guy in white, still standing across the road gazing lovingly in my direction. 'Oh, no!' he exclaimed. 'It's going to be like Thailand all over again.'

Over the course of the next month, similar things happened as we travelled through northern India. In Agra, a large group of people followed me around a market in a swarm, discussing amongst themselves whether I was or wasn't some famous, local actress. On a long, overnight train journey, I was spooked by a serial stalker, who seemed to think it would be quite alright to fondle my breasts while I slept. 'You no worry, *Memsahib*. Sleep, sleep!' Yeah, right!

I developed a strong desire to beat perfect strangers over the head just for staring at me. And an obsessive craving to blend in, to be unobtrusive, whatever that meant in a country where I was so obviously a foreigner. It was a long couple of weeks before I got the opportunity.

In a marketplace underneath Connaught Circus in Delhi, I ventured into a clothing shop staffed by three young men in impeccable turbans. The two that approached me spoke perfect Indian English, punctuated with broad, toothy smiles and much head wobbling. The single purpose of my foray into the world of local retail fashion was to find relief from the constant visibility I felt in Indian society. The single purpose of the two salesmen was to sell me the most ornate, brightly-coloured, glittery, tacky, expensive sari in the shop. It was never going to come to a happy end for all of us.

Salesman Number One ran off at the mouth with inane pleasantries, while Salesman Number Two fetched and carried ridiculous numbers of saris, *salwars* and *kurtas* for my approval. When I repeated my desire for something less decorative, something I could wear every day, they insisted this was it. When I protested that I wanted to just blend in, Salesman Number One moved closer to me and whispered furtively in my ear, '*Memsahib*, you will never just blend in.'

To their common disdain and disappointment, I did find a suitable cotton garment in mission brown and white, dowdy enough to be boring and priced well below their expectations. I bought two and wore one every day for the rest of our time in India.

It turned out they were right. It didn't help.

SEVEN

The Curse of Indian English

IN THE SAME BORDER TOWN in which I was presented with the rose by a perfect stranger, we had a very early bus departure for Varanasi via Patna. After the arduous journey down from Kathmandu, and the race back and forth across the border in a horse and cart to try and change money right on bank closing time (enough said), dinner and bed was all we could think about.

Now, you could be forgiven for thinking that someone who would walk miles at two in the morning to score a curry from the best Indian restaurant in town would be in culinary heaven in India. But like so many things on the subcontinent, when craving the familiar, disappointment reigned supreme.

Proudly displayed outside restaurants not much larger than a hole in the wall, extensive menu boards announced the mind-boggling variety of foods available within. But the English used to describe the dishes was as mangled as the dishes themselves. There was also the issue of trying to make ourselves understood when ordering these delicacies. It seemed that some simple words could be pronounced hundreds of different ways, yet still make absolutely no sense to Indian ears.

Case in point.

There was a clean-looking, pop up takeaway right next door to our Raxaul hotel. All we wanted was some dal and rice. Everyone has heard of dal, right? Especially the Indians in India, who eat it for almost every meal, right? But, no. So, when the young man behind the counter of this border town restaurant asked me what I wanted, I said in plain English/Hindi, 'Dal, please.' It was the only word I could have used. In return, I got one of those inimitable head wobbles and a blank stare. I said it again, louder, 'Dal.' Still nothing. Again, and again, and again, with different inflections, at various pitches, louder and louder. Nothing. Not the slightest hint of recognition of the word. I felt my blood pressure rise steeply.

Oh. My. God. This was my first day in India. I hadn't even made it 200 metres south of the Nepalese border and already I was frustrated to the max. I began to wonder about the wisdom of the trip. Maybe I wasn't cut out for India. Maybe I wasn't ready for it. Maybe I was going to loathe and detest every minute of it. Not even 200 metres south of the border I was beginning to regret my choices and question my motives. How was I going to be after a few weeks?

Finally, the man standing beside me at the counter said, in perfect English, no differently to how I'd said it, 'She wants dal.'

'Oh, dal?' The penny finally dropped. My rescuer looked embarrassed, and I felt like I'd stepped into an episode of *The Twilight Zone* and no one would ever understand another word I said. So, this was how it was going to be, then. For the next two months, I was going to be followed around and ceremoniously handed roses by men who couldn't understand a word I said. And stalked on trains by others who thought that I would be quite happy to be groped while I slept. Excellent. This was not a great start. But I had to steel myself against the possibility that I was not going to enjoy this country at all. I was going to have to fight for just about everything, including what I considered basic human rights. And then it dawned on me.

Welcome to India, *Memsahib*.

EIGHT

Transport Shock

AT SOMEWHERE AROUND 2 A.M. the next morning, we left Raxaul on a bus that would never have passed a road worthiness test. We were headed for Varanasi, but had to change modes of transport in the city of Patna. It was a very rough trip, uncomfortable and bumpy, and all night long the blasting of air horns from the impatient drivers sharing the road shattered any attempts at sleep.

Somewhere around a village called Muzzafaphur, I had my first real chance to reflect on the experience so far. Not that we had gone very far, but it seemed as if the whole earth had moved, twisted on its axis and launched me into another reality. For a short time, there had been no other vehicles on the road, so the air horn had remained quiet. I watched the sun rise through the bus windows. It was huge and crimson because of all the dust hovering in the air above the flatness of the landscape. It was like a painting from one of my treasured travel books. Not real. In my mind, I also heard a *sitar* wailing, but I think that was just me trying to make some music out of the incessant noise of the night before, shocked by the brief silence. India woke up that morning to the promise of another day of heat and sweat. And I awakened to the knowledge that, for now at least, this was my reality. My choice. For better or worse. Little did I know it was going to get a lot worse.

Patna turned out to be the armpit of the Earth, or that was how I perceived it in my naivety about the real India. Creased and irritable, we had to enlist the help of a waiting rickshaw *wallah* to get from the bus station to the train station. Even there we were duped, and the two tickets we thought we had purchased for a comfortable express train to Varanasi turned out to be a passport to hell.

When the train finally arrived, already two hours late, we discovered we would be spending the next seven hours jammed just below the ceiling of a second-class unreserved carriage, licensed to carry 72 seated/sleeping passengers, with 300 other people. If you're thinking second class couldn't be that bad, you've obviously missed the fact that this was an unreserved carriage. That meant no regulations, no luggage limit, and if you could get in the door or window, you could travel with anything. The locals seemed to be unable to travel without the kitchen sink. And the aluminium trunks and packages tied up in cloth and string did look big enough to hold one. These, of course, were too big to fit through the doors, so they were manhandled in through the open carriage windows onto the laps of those 'lucky' enough to get a seat.

Passengers trying to get from A to B weren't the only train travellers trying to board. The platform was teeming with hawkers of every kind of useless and unwanted gadget, knick-knack and dubious food item you could possibly imagine. Those men and women would jump the train as far as the next station and relentlessly sell their wares to their captive audiences. I don't know how many times I turned down rice treats wrapped in banana leaves, wooden flutes, plastic combs and unrecognisable things on skewers in those hideous seven hours. The only saving grace was that being on the top tier of the three-tiered sleeping platforms, we were above the intense action. However, it didn't stop the persistent and unwavering attempts to get the foreigners to buy something.

Those who weren't trying to sell us anything simply stared without blinking. For seven hours.

I don't think I ever got used to being stared at by unblinking eyes for hours on end. My every move seemed to be excruciatingly interesting, and I didn't get it. In fact, it annoyed the hell out of me. Sure, I was there, travelling on some esoteric premise of understanding how the other half lived. But was it possible that I was as intriguing to them as they were to me? We certainly had vastly different ways of expressing that intrigue. Mine was a more discreet method, or so I thought, observing from the sidelines, as it were. But they just stared. They didn't even try to hide it. It infuriated me, too, that their expressions were largely unreadable. I had no idea what they were thinking, whether they thought I was unusual, laughable, an idiot. Crazy even. Were they even making any judgements about me, as I so self-righteously was about them? I would never know the answer. And over the next couple of months, it would drive me insane.

By the time we hit Varanasi, at around midnight, we weren't in the mood for any more crap. But, hello, this was India. There was always crap to deal with, even at midnight. After a lot of arguing, somehow we convinced yet another rickshaw *wallah* that we really didn't want to go to the expensive Tourist Bungalow, and found a hotel still open that came with 'bed tea'. Whatever that was, the proprietor obviously thought it was a huge selling point for his run-down establishment.

Bed tea turned out to be a steaming pot and two cups delivered by over-exuberant staff members directly into the room at 6 a.m. the next morning. Having only gotten into bed well after 2 a.m., it was not appreciated to its full extent. The fact that the two young men who served it simply unlocked the door and entered our room didn't go down that well either. If I had been even half awake, I'm sure I would have shouted abuse at them. But I wasn't. I barely managed to open my eyes. When they left the room, we didn't surface again till midday.

And we cared not a jot that the bed tea went cold on the bedside tables.

NINE

Holy Crap

BY MIDDAY, OUR 'BED TEA' ROOM HAD HEATED up to an unbearable temperature that no longer allowed sleep to prevail. The bed tea still sat where it had been left five hours ago, and was now lukewarm again. A few bugs had decided that it might be a place to cool down. And drowned. It was a common theme in Varanasi. People came here to die. And that made for one hell of a mess.

The city was built on the banks of Mother Ganges, the sacred Hindu river, and Varanasi was famed for its river banks, or *ghats*. I had read in a guide book that being cremated on the steps of the *ghat* known as Marnikarnika offered a free ticket to the afterlife. No more reincarnation required. After witnessing firsthand the trials and tribulations of so many of the population, I could totally understand why this might be appealing. But with up to 300 cremations a day, you couldn't go too far without walking headlong into a funeral procession.

On our first trip outside the hotel, our 'greenness' must have betrayed us, and we managed to wind up in one of the ubiquitous silk show rooms that abound in Godaulia, the older part of the city. Spurred on by the promise of commissions just for getting unsuspecting tourists such as us into the shops, every rickshaw *wallah* in sight was eager to ferry us around for the day. It wasn't that bad an experience - the first time we were captured. The carpets and cloths were beautiful, and we were served *chai* and treated like royalty. Until we expressed the need to depart without buying anything. Just one visit was enough to savour the experience, but we got to do it several times over, just to be sure we didn't need any handmade rugs. As if the fact that they wouldn't have fit in our backpacks wasn't enough of a deterrent.

The winding maze of lanes and alleyways leading to Varanasi's Golden Temple were lined with stalls selling everything from incense and perfume oils, to food, *saris*, t-shirts, sweets and *chai*. And crowded with people, dogs, cows, rickshaws, and funeral processions. It was confronting, and a relief to come out into the open air by the river and breathe it all out.

Swollen by the monsoon rains, the Ganges of Varanasi was miles wide and flowing like a slow, majestic torrent. Still, we wanted to get out in a boat at sunrise and get another perspective on the city. So, we were hired by one of the boatmen for a leisurely cruise up and down the current. I say 'we were hired' because it didn't seem that we had much control over the entire transaction. But we were willing participants and easily manipulated.

Just before dawn on our third morning in India, we stood on the appointed meeting spot waiting for our boatmen. When we set off, the sun was hiding in the cloud and haze, at times a few rays breaking through to bathe everything in a magical, golden light. The river was high over the *ghats* and flowing very quickly, so rowing upstream was extremely difficult. Where it was cascading over the steps on the banks, it was a force to be reckoned with. Our two guides struggled fearlessly with the oars, battling the river with white knuckles on every stroke.

The float back to Marnikarnika was leisurely and mystical, the shoreline of the City of Light softened and made distant by the fine haze left after the day before. We all sat in silence and awe as the river picked us up and transported us downstream on the current. The rabble on the *ghats* was forgotten, just timeless echoes from another reality. The wailing of a *sitar*, real or imagined, poured out all the joys and sorrows of life in India across the cosmos. I was a privileged onlooker, stirred for a moment by passion for a people and a country where both the ancient and the infinite were mutually inclusive concepts. Temporarily, I forgot how I hated the place sometimes. I was filled with peace and love, like a true flower child. It was unrealistic, but it was real for a moment.

This love-hate relationship was a theme that constantly wove itself around my experiences in India. Things went right. Things went wrong more often. For an educated woman, raised to believe in equality and justice, India just didn't comply. My mind railed against the unfairness, injustice, and inequality that I found almost everywhere I turned. How could I overlook this? How could I make allowances for this twisted version of reality? Why should I try? It wasn't really my problem. I could leave at any time, go back to where I came from. Back to where things worked as they should, or at least worked more often than not.

But I would never be able to forget India. It affected me on a deep level. And it offended me. That's why I got so angry when things went wrong. It wasn't meant to be like that. It wasn't meant to be so hard. Not in my world.

But I wasn't in my world any more. I was in theirs.

TEN

Temple Porn

ON OUR LAST DAY IN THE HOLY CITY, we couldn't resist one last visit to the *ghats* before we left for Khajuraho, in the centre of northern India. We were still naive enough about Indian modes of transport to think that the upcoming train journey would be short and sweet, and that we had time for luxuries such as last-minute sightseeing. We had managed to secure second-class reserved seating for the seven-hour train trip to Satna. From there, we would take an open-backed, canopied jeep to the village famous for its temples adorned with so much 'pornography.'

As a newbie to the nuances of Indian train travel, I thought a window seat would be just the ticket. And that it was good to have such a firsthand view of the landscape that passed by as the train dawdled across the countryside, stopping frequently for no apparent reason. But I couldn't have been more wrong.

At every tiny junction and village station, I was beset by hawkers and beggars. The latter all had similar stories of woe and misfortune, and I'm sure they all deserved my empathy. But there were just too many. One poor old soul latched onto my forearm, which was resting on the open window sill, and would have dragged me from the train, I'm sure, had it not been for the horizontal steel bars. I began to fear for her safety when she refused to relinquish her grasp, even as the train began to pull away from the platform. It was impossible to remain unmoved by the pitiful faces pressing themselves to the bars on the windows, and it was especially difficult looking into the eyes of the children and the elderly. No matter how much I wanted to, I couldn't help them all, and helping even one was problematic in its own way, when the others got wind of the handout.

I began to be almost immune to the overwhelming number of people in need. But then we stopped at a tiny station somewhere near Satna. I had had my SLR and zoom lens pointed out the window of the carriage for some time, capturing random landscapes as we passed by. A teeming platform presented a massive opportunity for close-up portraits.

At the bottom of a set of stairs leading off the platform, lay a young girl. She stood out in my field of view because she was clad from head to toe in clean, white cloth which seemed to glow in the sunlight. A man and a woman squatted beside her body. They weren't begging. They weren't moving. They simply squatted, staring at the tiny, white form at their feet. Neither of them had noticed my lens. The shot was perfect. Then slowly, simultaneously, they both turned their heads and looked directly into the lens. The unbelievable sorrow in their eyes brought tears to my own. I knew their pain. It hurt my heart. And I could not take the photo.

For a long time after that, I couldn't look at the beggars. No matter how they beseeched me, I could not meet their gaze. Or even speak. I sat in silence, head bowed, the camera in my lap. How minuscule my woes and worries were compared to what I had just witnessed. How dare I moan and groan about the discomforts I had brought upon myself; asked for with my own choices. How humbling that fleeting glance. I could not remain unchanged. By the time we reached Satna, I was less a foolish girl, and more a mature woman.

The three-hour road trip from Satna to Khajuraho took us through Panna National Park, a lush rain forest, moist and green from the recent rains, and thickly carpeted in clover. So different from the India I had seen so far. When we stopped for short breaks, children came from everywhere, some wanting to practice their text book English, others just standing in the background, wide-eyed and staring. They seemed to be living in a veritable oasis in the heart of India. But as I learnt so brutally on the train earlier that day, looks could be deceiving.

If you only took a brief glance at it, the Bharat Lodge in Khajuraho looked like an okay place to stay. It measured up against other places we had stayed so far. But after such long journeys to get anywhere, by the time you got there you didn't care what the place looked like, as long as you could lie down. So, we chose here, in the heart temple town.

There were no real issues until they turned on the outside lighting in the evening. We were seated at long thin tables waiting for our dinner to be served when the lights went on. Almost instantly, thousands of black beetles swarmed us. They landed in our hair, our sleeves, our shoes. They went crazy for the lights. When our dinner arrived, they flew into our *sambal*. And drowned. Unfortunately, the bowls weren't big enough to make a dent in the population. Getting back into our room was like trying to outrun a fog. And once we were inside, I had to keep a towel at the foot of the door to keep them out. It didn't work. They squeezed in between the door and the jamb, dying for the light. It was like a scene from a bad horror film.

That was the thing about India, though. As beautiful as the scenery could be, and as colourful as the people were, there was always something worthy of complaint. Travelling around India was the greatest exercise in letting go. Either let go or go insane trying to hang onto basic western 'entitlements'. There wasn't any point. Nothing was going to change just because I didn't like it. It had likely been that way in India long before the Raj ever discovered and colonised it. And it would no doubt remain hostage to its teeming population and ancient rituals for a long time to come. Success was simply staying alive.

The temples of Khajuraho were magnificent. We hired old clunker bikes and rode out to see them. The Western Group, bar one, were all contained within a walled enclosure of well-kept paths and gardens. They were in remarkable condition, ornately carved from top to bottom, depicting figures going about daily life at that point in history. It was amazing to sit on the stone steps at the base and reflect on the fact that this building had stood here, just as it was now, for a thousand years. And to think that it had been put together atop massive stone platforms that once protruded from a lake. They were like giant jigsaw puzzles, fitting together without mortar or cement.

Apparently Khajuraho had seen its share of voyeurs, and some of the erotic carvings had been damaged. That didn't stop the over-zealous, self-appointed temple guides from steering all visitors toward the explicit scenes. They would point them out then nod and smile, all the while chanting, 'Sexy. Sexy.' It was disturbing, but in their minds, this is what we had come to see, not merely to enjoy the peace and quiet always so hard to find in India.

There was one temple that lay outside the compound, and it was still actively used by the locals. After a quiet weekend, on this Monday morning the town suddenly erupted into a bustling market place, with thousands of sari-clad women and white dhoti-dressed men thronging the steps of the outlying temple. They seemed to be paying homage to a large stone penis, the Shiva *lingam* housed inside. They emerged from the dark interior to the beat of bells, gongs and drums, completely drenched in water from the holy shrine. Several women circled a *pipal* tree which stood on the lower platform, making offerings of flowers at its base. The air was filled with frenzy and noise, a stark comparison to the calm and quiet inside the walled section. We stayed for a couple of hours, watching the colourful spectacle from the shade of one of the enormous old trees.

Dinner that night was yet another *thali*, served with the ubiquitous black beetles. They didn't help me to muster any semblance of an appetite for another average rendition of rice and dal. I kept thinking of thick slices of sourdough toast, with cheese and tomato. And with each thought, the meal in front of me grew less inviting. I picked over it for a polite length of time, spending more time rescuing bugs than finding spoonfuls that were free from insect life. In the end, I just gave up, gathered several towels and most of my clothes to barricade the bottom of the door, and went to bed. Tomorrow at dawn, another bone-rattler bus would deliver us westward, towards Agra and The Taj.

ELEVEN

Anywhere in Agra

FOR SOME INDECIPHERABLE REASON, ALL INDIAN BUSES seem to set out at dawn. The journey from Khajuraho to Agra was no exception. From 5:30 a.m. we were treated to the sheer joy of air horns, brakes and loud, loud Bollywood music. Five and a half hours of pure delight later, we arrived at the railhead of Jhansi, only to find the train to Agra was running two hours late. Oh, the absolute enchantment I felt at the prospect of breathing in the exquisite aromas of an Indian railway station for the next three hours while we waited for the train to arrive. I almost threw up with excitement.

But wait we did. And we managed to get a seat on the damn thing even without a reserved seat ticket. I think the Gods knew I had had just about enough. It all went downhill from there, though, when we finally arrived in Agra.

By the time our train pulled into the station, just on dark and more than four hours late, we had been in India long enough to be travel weary but not quite travel wise. We had travelled third class on buses and trains that departed at all hours of the day and night. And it didn't seem to matter what time it was, the same high pitched music and wailing streamed over the passengers at unspeakable volumes. This had the effect of turning a twelve-hour trip into a living hell. Relief came with arrival; at least, we still thought it was supposed to.

We alighted directly onto the railway tracks and were instantly swallowed up by a crowd of transport options. Representatives of all forms of carriage known to man were offered to us with the same hook – 'Anywhere in Agra for two rupees!' Having roughly three weeks' experience in bargaining for rides, this sounded like a good deal, even in a bicycle rickshaw. But the taxi drivers were all offering the same deal. It was a no-brainer. All that remained to do was to choose a driver.

The taxi was a chunky old Ambassador, big enough in the back seat for us and both our packs. No sooner had the door closed than the driver began babbling. Guttural sounds flowed from his lips like water, but not one single word could be understood. When he stopped at the entrance to Agra's flagship of the local hotel chain, his ploy slowly became apparent. He was taking us to *this* hotel in Agra for two rupees, not the one we wanted to go to, which was much further away. He would get a small commission for his efforts, *baksheesh*, and he was most determined. As he continued dribbling words, I tried to argue with him, saying over and over, louder and louder, the name of the hotel at our destination. He ignored me, so I just got out of the car, still stopped in the middle of the road with its right-hand indicator flashing. We both got out of the car. With our packs.

I was fired up now and ready to do a mean deal to get to the hotel, which we had picked for its proximity to the Taj Mahal. Waiting at the gates of this fancy hotel were several bicycle rickshaw *wallahs*. All of them had watched the argument in the taxi and witnessed its outcome. One of them sheepishly pushed his contraption towards us, as if he really didn't want to.

'Did you see that? Did you see what happened?' I fumed. 'Yes, Memsahib.' His head wobbled as he agreed.

'We want to go to the Shah Jahan Hotel. Will you take us there?'

'Yes, Memsahib.' More wobbling.

'For two rupees?' Only wobbling. We climbed up onto his 'rickety-shaw'.

This tiny, sinewy man wove skilfully in and out of the other road users, which included random cows, monkeys, chickens, parents and children, roaming salesmen with sky high trees of flutes and small stuffed toys, buses overflowing with passengers, motorbikes with three a seat, cars, and other bicycle rickshaws. Apparently, his riding skills were too advanced for his equipment, and before we had gone more than five hundred metres, the frame of his bicycle suddenly snapped into two distinct pieces — him with the handlebars and front wheel, and us with everything behind him. Unceremoniously, and in full public view, we slid forward and off the canopied seat on top of our luggage between the two pieces. Unbelievable. I paid him his two rupees because I felt sorry for him. He acknowledged my concern with just one wobble of his head.

It took some time and was almost dark by the time we managed to flag down an auto-rickshaw. Now we just wanted to get there by the quickest means. It was all too much. But still it wasn't to be a direct journey. The vehicle was almost out of gas, so when another babbling driver pulled into what looked to be a gas station, we had to pay our fare upfront so the driver could buy petrol. We had no real knowledge of where we were any more. Fortunately, the driver did then proceed directly to the door of our home for the next week.

As if by some small compensation for the day, our night was big and comfortable, with a low bed and lots of cushions for lazing about and reading. There was a small window/balcony onto the street below, and unbeknown to us, in the morning we would watch the sun rise over the stunning, white marble dome of the Taj Mahal.

TWELVE

The Taj

NOTHING COULD HAVE PREPARED ME for the beauty that is the Taj. It's huge white domes soaring majestically skyward, it stood at the end of a tree-lined water course, a symmetrically perfect monument to the passion of one man for his beloved wife. The biggest drawback were the crowds that flocked there each day, so it was a huge bonus to be staying in a guest house just metres from the main gates. I went there each morning at sunrise just to be one of the first inside. And one day, I was alone inside it.

The silence was overwhelming. There was a quiet hum that belonged to the building alone. Although a sign at the main gates requested quiet within the marble dome, few were able resist the childish temptation to test out its awesome acoustics by making loud cooee calls. They echoed around the chamber till no one could hear themselves think. Being the only one there was a gift.

I couldn't shake the overwhelming feeling that I had been here before, standing in these hallowed halls, breathing in the atmosphere. I've always been seduced by the doctrine of reincarnation. It didn't seem to me a completely unlikely event. Not that I thought I had once paraded myself around in the garb of Mumtaz Mahal, the great love of Emperor Shah Jahan's life, and for whom this edifice had been raised. No, nothing like that. But I felt a strange sense of knowing where I was, and I appreciated the gorgeous marble building from a far deeper place.

That feeling was probably why I was so appalled by the graffiti. Not ugly, spray-painted lettering six feet tall, but small inscriptions etched into the marble - 'Ram was here', and the like. It left a lingering sadness for such wanton disregard of the beauty of the Taj. The marble was already under attack from human pressures. The burgeoning industrialisation of the area had brought with it pollution that was quietly eating away at the building. How ironic, that a monument that had survived for over 300 years might fall victim to progress in a land where that progress would likely leave behind more people than it lifted out of poverty and despair.

Another building in the Jamuna river basin was destined to change our lives - the deserted city of Fatephur Sikri. We breathed in the wonderful views from our vantage point, seated on the high, red stone parapets looking out across the vast, flat plains. The remains of the great walled city were a curious blend of Muslim and Hindu architecture. Right in the middle of the complex was a mosque. Beside the main door there was a marble, lattice work window on which many bright red ribbons had been tied. According to legend, when Emperor Akbar successfully fathered three sons after praying in this mosque, those hoping for a son of their own began to make the pilgrimage here to pray. And so began the tradition of the red ribbons.

'Come, come,' urged one of the men standing by the door. 'Tie a ribbon. You will have a son.' For a small donation, he offered James one of the ribbons. James took the ribbon and tied it to the lattice.

Ten months later, and several years earlier than we had planned, our son was born. We called him Mani, after the Sanskrit word for jewel.

Om Mani Padme Hum. Hail to the jewel in the lotus.

THIRTEEN

Hail Ganga Ma!

THE BEATLES PUT RISHIKESH FIRMLY ON THE MAP a couple of decades before we got there in August of 1983. But for us, it was just another place from which to jump into the Himalaya. Perhaps it was the bad experience in the Tourist Bungalow food hall, where we had waited two hours to be served the same dish that was being delivered in large quantities to the 'real' pilgrims visiting the area. Or maybe it was the horse-drawn rickshaw ride that nearly ended in a bovine disaster at a busy intersection. But we decided to try a trek to the source of the Ganges. Because that's what 'real' pilgrims do? God only knows!

It wasn't the best decision considering we were smack bang in the heart of the rainy season. The narrow roads that wound through the mountain villages were prone to landslides and rockfalls that stopped all through-traffic. It also seemed that half of India was trying to make the trip with us, and most of them were very curious as to why we were there at all. It was terrifying at times, like when the edge of the road suddenly disappeared from under the bus. Or when the driver put his foot down to get through a dodgy part of the road as quickly as possible. Or when someone on the bus tried to move, there being about 70 people crammed into the tiny space.

The road to Lanka followed a steep, narrow valley, its sides covered with pine trees, small shrubs, firs, and marijuana plants. They grew shoulder high like weeds, no pun intended, all along the side of the road. On the floor of the ravine, Mother Ganges hurtled towards the Indian plains, a powerful force even so close to its source.

The road was extremely treacherous and only just wide enough for the bus. I tried not to think about what might happen if we met another vehicle, even a motorbike. Each time the bus traversed a potentially life-threatening patch of roadway, the pilgrims cheered. 'Hail, Ganga Ma!' Not surprisingly, we eventually reached a roadblock that defied further passage. Slowly, oh so slowly, we all disembarked, waited for our luggage to be retrieved from the roof, and walked across the massive landslide.

It was tricky, since rocks and dirt were still tumbling down the mountain side, and in places, we had to run. Once on the other side, it was another five kilometres to the next roadblock and the bus that had come from our destination to collect us. Fortunately, it seemed to have survived the 50-point turn required to retrace its route before we got there.

The entire journey from Uttarkashi took over 14 gruelling hours. As the only foreigners making the trip, we had been objects of intense scrutiny for most of that time. But luckily for us, a group of tourists from West Bengal, a family unit with excellent English, befriended us. They helped us to find a place to lay our sleeping bags on the floor of one of the many tents that passed for accommodation in Lanka. After that, it was easy to find sleep.

Early the next morning, we learnt we had to walk about two kilometres to the village of Bhaironghati, from where we could catch a jeep to Gangotri. The road between the two villages was little more than a goat track, one kilometre down to a river, and another kilometre up to the village. Some of the more elderly pilgrims opted for the human taxi service - a thin, wiry porter with a tumpline around his forehead, attached to a basket containing the passenger. It looked uncomfortable for both parties. Even so, I wished that I was about 20 kilograms lighter, so that I, too, might have been spared the horrendous walk.

After tea, biscuits and a visit to the local temple with our newfound friends, we finally left Gangotri for the 13-kilometre trek to Baba Lal's ashram at Bhojbhasa, altitude 3,500 metres. The path took us up, slowly at first, through pine and fir forests, and across cascading streams. The gradient was casual, but we emerged from the forests into the rugged loneliness that is glacial country, with no shelter from the burning midday sun. In the rarefied atmosphere, it was taxing. And stinking hot.

Throwing caution to the wind, we stopped often and drank frequently and fearlessly from the streams that crossed our paths, making their way to join the Ganges below us. At several such stops, I lay spreadeagled on my backpack like a giant upturned beetle unable to right itself. I laughed at my lack of fitness, and how ridiculous I might have looked to anyone passing by. Not that there was much foot traffic up here. But every now and then, as if to offer incentive, the clouds over the peaks parted just enough to show us the snow-covered, rocky massifs that overlooked our paths.

It took seven toiling hours to reach our destination by the early evening. Baba Lal's ashram was little more than a series of open-walled tents with various areas assigned to cooking, cleaning, meditating and sleeping. We'd arrived too late for the evening meal, so it was lucky that we were too exhausted to care about food. That would come the next morning.

We woke early to find a chill wind blowing across the valley. Our fellow pilgrims had mostly already left on the last upward part of the journey to Gaumukh, the mouth of the Ganges. By the time we arrived there, the sky had cleared. But the sun had heated the snow just enough to send a veil of mist rolling over us. Our friends were already drying themselves off from their ritual bath in the icy water, and greeted us as they shivered in their wet loin cloths.

The river issued from the bowels of an ice cave in the Gangotri Glacier, a raging brown torrent that sent huge ice blocks plummeting down the river. I'd seen the damage the river could do on the plains, swelled by the monsoon rains, as it meandered, vast and majestic, toward its delta in the Bay of Bengal. Standing alone on the edge of one of the many cliffs, not a soul in sight as far as the eye could see, Mother Ganges at my feet, I felt very small and insignificant. I realised I could believe anything I wanted about my life, because here it made no difference to anyone or anything. There was only me and the mountains in my field of view, blended into one past, present and future. Only now had any meaning.

It was a 23-kilometre walk back down the mountains to yet another ashram before we could get anything to eat. This one was more established, being far less remote than Baba Lal's, and they fed us to the eyeballs. In fact, we were overfed and couldn't quite finish the huge *thali* plates before us. Unsure what to do with the leftovers as we washed up our plates in the ashram kitchen, we took the sodden scraps back to our room and hurled them onto the unsuspecting marijuana plants lurking just outside our window. It seemed fitting at the time.

Sadly, a couple of years after our visit, a major earthquake demolished the village of Uttarkashi. It had been such a pretty place, especially at night, when all the street stalls lit up their incandescents and candles. Uncommonly in India, it was clean. Even the streets were spotlessly swept. There was an obvious communal pride in play. It had a homely and inviting atmosphere, and the people were the same. Maybe it helped that few foreigners made it this far into the Indian Himalaya, most opting instead for the more well-worn trails of Nepal. An old man had chased us up the stairs of our hotel as we were returning after dinner one evening just to remind us that we had met him in Gangotri. He didn't want anything more than to make an impression. It was endearing.

We had planned to make our next destination the northern most state of Jammu and Kashmir. But the monsoon conspired against us and took out the road to Srinagar. So, we ended up back in Rishikesh. After the peace and quiet of the mountains, even this smallish city was too noisy and crowded for our liking. We decided on Dharamsala, or more precisely, McLeod Ganj, home-in-exile of the Dalai Lama.

After spending a couple of days exploring the hill station of Shimla, popular with the British Raj, we made our way north through Himachal Pradesh. Perched high on a ridge above Dharamsala, the population of McLeod Ganj was mostly Tibetan. There was a monastery, a lot of saffron-clad monks, and an extensive Buddhist library. There was also a colourful mix of foreigners, all looking to kick back and savour the atmosphere. Some had even set up house in the surrounding hills and had been there for quite some time. It was easy to get lost in enclaves like this one, peaceful retreats from the 'real' India. Yet, still a part of India.

I, too, found my paradise there, and another place I never wanted to leave. I had always had a keen interest in natural medicine, and when I discovered the School of Tibetan Medicine on a walking path below the village, it became my one aim in life to study there. Of course, it was a totally unrealistic goal, since I couldn't speak Tibetan. That was a prerequisite. Still, it didn't stop me from exploring every angle to try to find a loop hole. There weren't any. It wasn't going to happen. So instead, I had to content myself with hanging out at the library, ploughing through Buddhist literature and soaking up the vibes.

The cafes and restaurants catered well to the transient tourist population. It reminded me of the Kathmandu scene. There were a few faces who looked like they would never leave. And some that should probably never have come. It was easy to get caught in the backwater, to forget the rest of the world existed. And the low cost of living fuelled the temptation to stay.

James' and my relationship finally found the time to heal more permanently in McLeod Ganj. Maybe that contributed to the length of time we stayed there. Constantly moving, sleeping in single dormitory beds, living out of a backpack, sharing rooms with other travellers - it's just not conducive to intimacy. Relationships lived on the road are strengthened in other ways. Any traveller knows that. We got to see another side of each other, one we might never have seen at home in suburbia; the side that deals with stress, frustration and sometimes, bitter disappointment. I'm not saying it could never have happened in other situations, but travelling together for an extended period of time brought it to the fore. Staying in the one spot for so long, in a place where the atmosphere was laid back and relaxed, it was easier to rekindle respect and passion for each other.

It was also here, in McLeod Ganj, that I fell pregnant. Totally unplanned, and arguably not the best outcome, it was another trial to deal with in a country with untold trials. I blamed the red ribbon at the mosque in Agra, and the moon. I had been using a natural method of birth control based on the position of the moon at the time of my birth, and its relationship to the fertility cycle. Some time during the trip, I had screwed up the dates. It was bound to happen sooner or later. So, why not blame the moon? But even though it threw a few spanners our way, it felt right. It would most likely shorten our trip, and that caused some angst. We had set off from home on an open-ended journey. Babies weren't going to be part of the picture for at least ten years. We had already had that discussion. But we decided to carry on with our trekking plans anyway. As long as I could manage it. Time would tell.

If I had been a different woman, or ours a more typical marriage, I might have freaked out about a pregnancy so far from home. But as it was, I had begun to feel that I was at home wherever I was. I was learning to take responsibility for my choices, and that I alone had the power to make them. I confess, I didn't relish the thought of giving birth in India, but I had enough faith in the universe that things would work out 'somehow'. Many would have disagreed with that philosophy. Especially my family. And it certainly wasn't a choice without risk. But then very few worthwhile things in life are. The greater the risk, the greater the reward. You just have to be prepared to accept the consequences. Because there will be consequences.

So, wisely, as it turned out, we decided not to tell the family. Not yet, anyway. They would only worry. And they were already worried, without that added burden.

It was so relaxing; it took us a couple of weeks before we could drag ourselves away. But we needed to get back to Kathmandu in time for the trekking season. We had planned for the Annapurna and Everest treks. There were lots of preparations to make. Swanning around in an Indian hill station, eating sublime Tibetan food and getting fat just wasn't going to cut it. Damn it!

FOURTEEN

Random Drug Search

ON OUR DEPARTURE FROM MCLEOD GANJ, we opted for an overnight bus. The journey promised to be 12 or 13 hours of pure overnight hell. I had hoped that sleep might just visit its welcome self upon us for at least part of the journey. It didn't, and after 13 sleep-haunted hours and only one comfort stop, the crate they called a bus and its shattered and battered cargo ground to a halt at the Interstate Bus Terminal in Delhi. As with all good bus and train stations in India, it was miles from where we needed to be.

It was 4:45 am and still dark, but warm enough to foreshadow another hot day in the city. Zombie-like, we dragged ourselves and our bulging backpacks off the bus and into the waiting passions of about five enthusiastic rickshaw *wallahs*. Some of them seemed only able to understand English when it was screamed at them. In my mood that morning, it was easy to oblige. Even the saintly would find it difficult to remain calm after an extended period in India. They had the happy knack of making the simplest things confusing, time-consuming and frustrating.

After making certain the rickshaw driver understood that we really did want to go to Janpath, an area of cheap hotels on the outer fringes of central New Delhi, and not to the hotel that he thought we should be staying at, we set off. It was incredible how they always thought they knew better than us where we wanted to go. And even more amazing, that they thought they would be able to convince us otherwise.

Five minutes out of the bus station, a young boy on the side of the road flagged us down, promptly waved over a policeman, and then disappeared into the darkness. With the aid of a torch, because it was pre-dawn, the cop conducted a thorough search of all our luggage, first James' and then mine. I suddenly remembered that I may have forgotten to ditch a tiny ball of hash that I had stashed away in a small container for a friend we had met in the mountains. In only a slight panic, I opened my pack and located it, surreptitiously removed it while the other pack was being searched, and stuck it in my pocket. Unluckily for me, once the policeman had finished with my pack, he directed James to empty his pockets. Without breaking a sweat, I simply removed the tin from my pocket and replaced it in my backpack before I zipped it up. Then I took my turn to empty my pockets.

To this day, I still can't believe I did that. And so calmly. I could never have managed the sleight of hand in daylight. I'm terrible at deception, which is one of the reasons I never tell lies. That, and a staunch Christian father, who instilled the virtue of honesty in me from an early age. More than once it had gotten me into deep trouble with my friends. But that's another story.

Once the cop had determined that we had no drugs on us, he asked to see our passports. He scrutinised every page, searching for our visas. As Commonwealth citizens, we were not subject to visa requirements, and after pursuing that argument to the death, he was forced to admit that we were free to go. No *baksheesh* for him that morning.

Scenes like this occur randomly in third world countries, or anywhere corrupt officials like to supplement their meagre wages with tourist dollars. That night, we were too slippery for him. But a great lesson was learnt. It can happen any time, any place, when you least expect it, so - don't travel with drugs. Anywhere. Ever.

FIFTEEN

Blue Eyes Over Sonauli

OUR NEXT LONG AND ARDUOUS BUS TRIP from New Delhi to Kathmandu meant another early morning departure from the Tourist Camp. There were a handful of tourists, and a large group of Tibetan exiles trying to return home. When we arrived at 5 a.m., several men had formed a human chain from the ground to the roof of the bus, and were busy hauling up haystack-sized parcels wrapped in cloth and tied with endless amounts of string. It all belonged to the Tibetans, who, like the Indians, seemed incapable of travelling light. So many times I'd found myself safely settled into a second-class window seat on an Indian train, only to be assaulted and dislodged by the sharp end of a huge aluminium trunk injecting itself through the open window beside me.

When the bus was finally loaded with more luggage and passengers than seemed possible, we set off, lurching our way out of the bus station in fits and starts. The route took us back through Agra again. While the train trip from Agra to Delhi had taken a mere three hours on the Taj Express, by bus it took six. Add to this the two-hour delay to our departure and you have some idea of the state of us by the time we arrived at the Taj for lunch and sightseeing. It was the last time we got to eat for a couple of days. This troubled me more than a little, considering the baby I believed I was carrying through this hell.

The bus drove all day and night in the direction of Sonauli on the India-Nepal border, not once stopping for food or water until 40 kilometres the other side of Gorakhpur, just short of the border. The heat was hellish and the thirst unquenchable. More thvan once I wished that I could just pass out from heat exhaustion to escape it all.

When we finally reached the border post at around 10 p.m. on day two, it was about to close. The grumpy border guards, unhappy at being dragged away from their post right on closing time, refused to allow safe passage for the bus and any of its passengers without checking all the rooftop luggage. Unless the owners of the said luggage were amenable to paying some *baksheesh*. Three hundred rupees from each man, woman and child. Of course, they refused. The arguments on both sides continued for about half an hour, when it became obvious that the luggage WAS going to be inspected. But not tonight. We were all unceremoniously herded from the bus and pointed in the direction of the village to find a room for the night.

At that late hour, there was nowhere open to change money. We had about ten rupees between us, which may have gotten us something to eat, but came nowhere near the cost of a room. Things looked grim for a while, until a couple of our fellow passengers, who had witnessed our predicament, offered to loan us the money for a room. It wasn't much, but it made a huge difference to our states of mind. And saved us from having to sleep on the street. Sometimes, just sometimes, the gods were on our side.

The sun woke us up at dawn the next morning, streaming in through a window that had no covering of any kind. The heat quickly followed, making it impossible to sleep. We didn't have any luggage. It had remained on the bus. There was no point having a shower only to get back into clothes that pretty much stood up on their own. But we did it anyway. It didn't make me feel much better. It certainly didn't make me look any better.

When the exchange counter opened, we were at least able to change some money and pay for our visas, and repay the Spanish guys who had so generously helped us out the night before. But we still weren't able to leave. A whole new brigade of border officers was busy offloading the haystacks from the bus roof and rifling through them in search of contraband. After breakfast, we wandered off to look for some shade. It seemed there was only one tree in the whole of this village, and most of our fellow passengers had found it before us.

As we approached the gathering, I noticed one of the American ladies travelling with us was seated at the centre of the group. The others had arranged themselves in a circle around her. She was speaking quietly, telling a story about a meditation course she had just completed. I remember wondering whether that was the reason she seemed so composed in the face of our current situation. I also remember she had the bluest eyes I had ever seen, and looked beatific as she sat cross legged in the dirt and dust.

Then she said something that I have never forgotten: 'If you do only one thing for yourself in your lifetime, do this - a Vipassana meditation course.' It stuck with me, and in the following years, I did not one, but three ten-day courses. And each time, I was pregnant. They changed my life. Looking back now, it makes me think. You never know when or where you will find the tiny piece of the jigsaw that makes the picture complete. And the one who hands it to you may be the most unlikely. Without ever knowing it, she taught me to never take anything for granted. And I am eternally grateful to her whose name I don't even know.

Once we finally got approval to depart, the rest of the journey was more relaxed. We all felt like we knew each other a little better, and conversation flowed back and forth on the bus. The driver, too, seemed to have lost his desire to get to Kathmandu without stopping, and we all benefited from the now frequent comfort breaks. When we arrived in Kathmandu, it truly felt like we had come home. But best of all, we had survived India.

SIXTEEN

In the Shoes of a Trekker

THE MAIN REASON I WENT TO NEPAL WAS THE MOUNTAINS. The Himalaya. They loomed as every backdrop just on the rim of the Kathmandu Valley. When I first arrived, at the tail end of summer, they were shrouded in mist in the early morning and obscured by clouds for the rest of the day. But I knew they were there. We talked about them over endless rounds of coffee and cake in the cafes and traveller hangouts. We planned our treks while we waited for the weather to clear. They were the reward for the difficult bus trip to Pokhara, six and a half hours' drive to the west.

Treks leaving from Pokhara took in the Annapurna and Dhaulagiri ranges that formed the sides of the Kali Gandaki Valley, the deepest in the world at over 4,000 metres. The trails were supposedly easier than the trek to Everest Base Camp, especially the first few days out, and guided groups of all ages and nationalities frequented them.

Some trekkers were decked out to the nines, notably the groups of Japanese. They wore a uniform of shorts and shirts, with bandannas, water bottles, caps and good, solid boots. They carried their day packs and a sturdy stick. Their porters carried the rest in huge baskets secured on tumplines around their foreheads. They camped at night in pre-erected tents, set up by the sprightly porters who had somehow managed to reach the evening destination an hour before the first trekker in their party.

James and I carried our own bags, everything we needed for three weeks in the mountains. That included lots of toilet paper, and small change. They were so overwhelmingly heavy that half way through the first day, after climbing for just a few hours, we dumped our sleeping bags. After staggering red-faced into the walled yard of a small farmhouse sitting atop the ridge, a kind *didi* made us *chia*, a sweet boiled tea. As we paid her, we also negotiated the price of storing the sleeping bags till we came back down the trail. Her English-speaking son had convinced us that we would not need them on this trek. All the lodges were well equipped with blankets, so he said. We were easy prey. Fortunately for us, he was right, although our requests for blankets did meet with confused looks and questions about why we had no sleeping bags.

The lodges and inns that dotted the trail to Jomson and Muktinath, a pilgrimage site, were used to dealing with streams of foreigners. They had learnt to cook the food and provide the accommodation, even a hot shower here and there. And they did it well.

The food was glorious, all flavours and tastes. A guest house in Tatopani, five days' walk into the Annapurna, did the best fettuccine and lemon meringue pie in the world. The *rakshi*, local rice wine, was rough, but you generally didn't notice after the first couple of glasses. We played Euchre by candle light and talked into the night, swapping trail stories and addresses. We retired to small, stone rooms with beds and a blanket. If we slept in all our clothes, it was warm enough. Just.

Then the next morning we got up and did it again, another six or seven hours, walking through forests and climbing up rocks, across suspension bridges, and through tiny villages. We stopped frequently for tea and biscuits. We stopped even more often for photographs. The mountains excelled themselves with clear continuous views of their glacial faces, and brilliant sunsets.

At Deurali, perched on a pass at about 3,000 metres, we took a day out to do some washing. It didn't dry very well in the mist which hovered all day. A lovely pot belly stove in the middle of the restaurant did the trick though. We spent the day in there, sipping coffee and catching up on letters home. We debated the pros and cons of climbing Poon Hill, another 300 metres up behind the village, to catch sunrise over the Dhaulagiri range. But luckily, it rained all night, which meant another hours' precious sleep instead.

The rain was not so popular when we decided to leave on the downhill path to Tatopani. It was slippery and miserable, and an hour passed before we climbed down out of the fog. The night-long rain had also washed away a large section of the trail just past the village of Chitre, leaving a gaping sore across the mountainside. In parts below us, it was still moving. But we were not the first to pick our way cautiously across, probably about 100 metres in all. A rough trail of footprints showed the successes and the follies of those who had come before. So, we followed them.

After we passed through Kalopani, a village of just a few guest houses with kitchens, which stretched along a cobbled footpath, we climbed down from a narrow suspension bridge to the edge of a vast floodplain. The Kali Gandaki Valley spread out before us. Mind-blowing white peaks soared skyward from either side. The indistinct path seemed to head out straight across the river bed. Blindly, we followed it.

At the edge of one of the many streams traversing the expanse of gravel, the trail simply disappeared. It was impossible to see it taking up again on the other side, about ten metres across. For a bleak, rainy hour we wandered up and down the bank trying to find a spot with enough stepping stones to keep our feet dry. Hopeless, we reached the only conclusion. There were none. We would have to take our shoes off and brave the freezing water.

As we were wondering just how deep it was going to get, a band of porters came through behind us. They had no qualms about wading knee deep into the veritable rushing river. I watched them lurch haphazardly towards the other side, their heavy loads catching them off balance in the strong current.

For some insane reason, I thought I would be able to manage everything more safely if I threw something over to the other side. Stupidly, I threw one of my shoes. It landed, plop, and began sailing away downstream like hapless jetsam. One of the porters, already mid-stream, performed a series of slick manoeuvres and plucked it up as it passed close by him. In that small moment, images of the rest of the trek with only one shoe had flashed before my eyes. I think I screamed. Another porter grabbed my arm from behind and propelled me forward, much faster than I could have managed alone. And that was the only reason I made it across.

We caught up with all of them, sipping tea in yet another guest house. As we arrived, the conversation obviously turned to us and our river-crossing antics. Though I couldn't understand a word, I knew exactly why they were all laughing hysterically.

We spent that night in a newly-built room of stone blocks and pine windows in Marpha, having walked through drizzle all afternoon to get there. A largish village of paved alleyways and whitewashed houses, Marpha seemed to huddle. Almost every door off the neat, white alley hid a sunny courtyard, protected from the fierce winds that howled up the valley after 11 a.m. every day. Marpha was a tidy, white town. As if to add emphasis, it snowed all night.

We awoke to a weak sunlight cracking the icy glaze on the windows into myriad tiny lights. The tree outside bowed gracefully under the weight. The village was virtually invisible.

The winds added an extra touch of cruelty to the landscape in these high altitudes. It was beautiful, but forbidding. Jomsom was a disappointment, an outpost town spread out around a rudimentary airstrip and the river. It was eerie, empty, and windy. It was as if the wind had blown the place flat and the buildings apart from each other. No film could capture it. We blew in one end of it and blew out the other.

Though the village of Muktinath, just below a 5,000-metre pass, was the pinnacle of this trek, Kagbeni was the highlight. We approached the jumble of buildings and prayer flags on flat stony paths through a cluster of green and yellow terraced fields of maize. We strolled in early afternoon, surprisingly short of breath for the slow gradient up from Jomsom. The streets were empty of all but free-ranging cows, dogs and chickens.

As in Marpha, courtyards abounded behind thick mud and dung walls with heavy wooden doors. No coat of whitewash here, though. Many of the doors were padlocked, which gave the place an abandoned air. From the far side of the river, a gushing torrent now, the village looked as if it had been thrown there against the ridge with great force. The buildings leaned at odd angles, probably supporting each other, some succumbing to the desolate climate. All the roofs were flat, and many sported streamers of prayer flags. The wind had all but shredded them, but sent their messages towards the heavens with blistering fervour, nevertheless.

There was a large *gompa* on a rocky outcrop just north of the village. From this Buddhist monument, I could see a long way up the valley towards Mustang, a protected area of Tibet. Foreigners weren't allowed past this point without special permits, but just staring into the barren, unearthly, wind-blown landscape was humbling. When I looked back down at Kagbeni, I was transported to the Middle Ages, and rising in the background were the 7,000-metre peaks of the Annapurna, pinnacles of rock and ice. It was breathtaking.

On the way back into the village we passed a row of *mani* wheels. Tradition holds that they must be kept to the right, and each wheel spun in turn as you pass, chanting the mantra *'Om mani padme hum'*, roughly translated as 'Hail to the jewel in the lotus.'

An old woman and a man with two white eyes sat on the steps of a doorway, spinning their own personal prayer wheels. The woman smiled as we gave each wheel in the wall a good tug with our right hands. I wondered what she thought of us, if she wondered where we came from. In the remote Himalaya, Western society must have seemed a myth, perpetuated by a trickle of trekkers from all over the world. We all contributed to their image of us, good and bad. How did we look?

Such questions used to haunt me when I witnessed a confrontation between trekker and inn keeper or cook. These people opened their homes and called them lodges to attract the tourist dollar. Their kitchens became Western food factories, churning out meals suitable for the delicate foreign palate and even more delicate stomach. And sometimes, in return, they were treated with contempt. Arguing over what was, in the end, only a few cents for a meal or a room, or even the total of the bill, seemed lousy in anyone's language. Arguing over basic facilities or the lack of hot showers was just absurd.

The roof of every building was used as a storage and drying area for clothes, grains and wood. Looking at the barren slopes of the surrounding peaks, it was obvious the wood had been carried in from afar. Crucial not only for warmth, but also for cooking, there was none left to speak of in these parts. Many kitchens ran on the droppings of the family buffalo or yak.

Kagbeni made me think of things differently, like how much I took for granted, and what was important. Life was not easy in this environment, but it was simple. And it took place largely inside walled courtyards. People gathered in the streets for conversations and games only later in the day, when the wind had dropped a little. There was one shop selling everything from *bidis*, tiny Indian cigarettes rolled in a leaf, to blocks of Swiss chocolate, the latter at a premium, of course.

I imagined what it might be like, having to walk for days to get fuel to cook, or to buy groceries, and then carry everything home again. How long would ten kilos of rice last? How long would I last carrying it? How often would it need to be done? What if the river was the only source of fresh water? How would I feel about having access to only one measly little store?

We were so spoilt, growing up in a country where things happened at the flick of a switch or the turn of a tap; where everything was at our fingertips, or just a short car ride away. Yet we didn't even know it till we came here, or to a place like this, where people struggled every day, just to survive.

I realised that I, too, took these conveniences, and many more, for granted. Hell, I even saw them as a right, an entitlement. I moaned long and loudly when these conveniences failed, or failed to live up to my expectations. As a child, I had thrown tantrums if things didn't go my way; if my 'right' to watch television or visit a friend's house was denied. What a brat!

Wise men throughout history have said that you can only fully understand the wisdom of another by following in their footsteps. In Kagbeni, it dawned on me that travelling was all about wearing different shoes.

SEVENTEEN

No Running!

'I'M PRETTY SURE I'M PREGNANT.'

These were the words with which I greeted Doctor Dali when I finally got into her Kathmandu clinic after waiting several hours. I'd just spent three weeks trekking the Annapurna ranges in all kinds of pain. Several of my body parts had let me down badly - two crippled knees from bouncing downhill on large boulders, and a chest infection that made every breath painful.

A doctor in Pokhara had informed me I had mumps, and had prescribed enough pills to fill another backpack. Wary of his diagnosis, I asked the advice of a group of New Zealand nurses I met in the street. Showing them all the prescriptions I had in my hand, I asked, 'Would you take any of these if you thought you were pregnant?'

'Oh my God, no!' they chorused.

So I was in no mood for charlatans who had no idea what they were talking about. This lady doctor seemed to be different. She simply smiled at me and told me to get up on the bed.

After several minutes of pushing and poking my abdomen, listening with a stethoscope, and conducting an internal examination, she said, 'Yes. I think you might be pregnant. About seven weeks, I would say.'

The Annapurna trek had taken us three weeks, which meant that I was about four weeks pregnant when we started out.

She asked me lots of questions then, where I was from, when I had arrived in Kathmandu, where I was staying, how long I was going to stay, and why I had come to Nepal. When she learnt I was not going to be going 'home' any time soon, she asked why.

'I came to Nepal to trek, and that's what I plan to do. I've just done the Muktinath trek, and soon we're leaving for Everest Base Camp.'

Again she smiled, probably at my girlish naivety. That's when she said it. 'Well, walk if you must, but don't run.'

I'd never been pregnant before and my ignorance of all the changes that go along with the condition was probably what saved me from worrying about what might happen during three or four weeks in the remote Himalaya. My only guide to having a child was a book called *Everywoman* that I had managed to pick up in a local second-hand book store. It gave me the week-by-week basics and little else. I read it from cover to cover before our next trek.

Yet, despite having that book for my one and only guide, I still had no idea what to expect. I also had no idea what might go wrong. I didn't have time for it anyway, just like I didn't have time for morning sickness. Or to wonder what might be going on inside my belly. I had to walk more than 20 kilometres every day, from sun up till sunset, just to get where we were going. I never questioned that. I had already made that choice. Now it just had to be done.

Some days it was hard. We walked uphill for hours at a time, sometimes for the whole day. When I stopped to rest my backpack on one of the many stone platforms that strategically dotted the trail, I often didn't want to take up the weight on my shoulders again. I drank all the water in my hip flask long before there was going to be another chance to refill it. And I arrived in villages at the end of the day lathered in sweat and clothed in the dirty streaks of too much walking.

I had no idea what I looked like. There were no mirrors. And very few shower opportunities.

But one thing all that walking did allow was silence. Most of the time, my face was bent to the ground and my shoulders stooped, following the footsteps of those who had already passed that way. There were too many rocks and boulders ready to throw me off balance to lose concentration for even a minute. There was no breath for talking. I was alone with my thoughts for most of the day.

When you find yourself in a situation of your own making, when you must do hard things, you just do them. I would be lying if I said I wasn't angry sometimes, resentful that I had made the choices that made my life so difficult. But that was just the point. I had made those choices in full knowledge of the consequences. But it still pissed me off.

I learnt a lot of things about myself up there in the cold, inhospitable environment. I couldn't shake the feeling that I wasn't meant to be there. That none of us was meant to be there. It was such an alien place. And once more, I felt very small and insignificant amongst the massive rocks and ice flows.

But somehow it changed me inside. I was determined that the troubles and woes that beset me would not beat me. I had free will. I would prevail. I could have turned around at any point and refused to go any further. But I didn't. Why? Because I am nothing if not stubborn. I might have gone there blindly. But I came back with my eyes wide open.

EIGHTEEN

Pregnant Among the Peaks

NO ONE IN THEIR RIGHT MIND finds out they're seven weeks pregnant and then embarks on a three-week trek to Everest Base Camp, right?

Wrong.

To be honest, I didn't give it too much thought. If I had, I might have made a different decision. But I had no experience with pregnancy, no idea what to expect, and no time to think about the million things that could possibly go wrong. Those kinds of problems just weren't on my radar. Much more likely to get a second glance was anything that had to do with preparations for the trek - permits, sleeping bags, down jackets, decent hiking boots, small denomination notes, water purification tablets, and loads of toilet paper. These were the things that occupied my mind for the week prior to setting off on a day-long bus ride into the Himalayan foothills. Morning sickness? What was that?

In 1983, the trail head for the Khumbu region was far short of Jiri or Shivalaya, where it starts these days. Those roads just didn't exist back then, or at least, didn't connect up with each other. Even today, the last few hours on the road to Shivalaya is more like a boulder-strewn river bed than a road.

We took a bus to Lamosangu, just shy of the Tibetan border, without even making a booking. We just turned up at the bus station and got on a bus. The small town was the end of the paved road. When they hauled our backpacks down from the roof after we arrived, it was immediately obvious that someone had broken the zipper on mine, despite the padlock. I searched frantically to find out what was missing. It was my camera. I hadn't expected to be separated from my bag, but had declined to ride on the roof of the bus with many of the other passengers. It definitely would have been the more comfortable option. And I would still have had my camera. That was a bummer, starting out on a trek to Everest without the means to capture it for posterity. I was bitterly disappointed, and angry at myself for being so stupid as to pack my camera in my backpack. But I was brought up to treat others the way I would like to be treated. Naively, I trusted people; the wrong people. It was a hard lesson, and made me feel physically sick. Or maybe that was the hormones. Maybe 'baby brain' had kicked in early.

We were pointed in the direction of another form of vehicular transport that was going to convey us to Kirantichap, about where the road turned into a goat track. It was a van with a single back door that opened outwards, and very little inside in the way of seating. It looked ancient.

The sun had descended below the ridge when we set off up the steep, winding dirt road on the far side of the river. Before long it was dark. The road got progressively worse as we drove. I found myself getting bounced up and down on the hard wooden seat, which probably wasn't too good for me in the early stages of pregnancy. So I stood up and held tight to the overhead rail, keeping my knees bent just enough to soften the impact.

It worked okay for a while, until suddenly there was a roar from the driver's seat and the van began ducking and diving from side to side, off the road, back on the road, off the other side, until finally we screeched to a stop. One of the young boys opened the back door and leapt out, returning a minute later holding up what looked like a dead rabbit. Yes, the driver had managed to chase it down in a van full of passengers.

'Dinner!' he proclaimed, proudly. The Nepali passengers cheered and congratulated him. The foreigners shook their heads and looked sick. Seriously? Thank God it was dark and I hadn't been able to see how close each of these switchbacking manoeuvres had taken us to careening off the mountain.

Kirantichap was just a couple of buildings with a track through the middle of it. There was only one choice of a place to stay, so we stayed there, in the building to the left. The next morning we followed a rudimentary road out of town along a ridge, then descended into a thick forest of firs. If we had asked around in Kirantichap, or waited just a little longer before leaving, we probably could have hitched a ride on a local pickup. Despite being dangerous and poorly formed in many places, the road was passable. So, a few hours later, when just such a pickup came along, we got in the back with a couple of locals and rode all the way to Jiri for 15 rupees, about fifty cents each.

We found ourselves in a lodge with a team of disorganised mountain climbers for companions. They intended to climb one of the lesser Khumbu peaks not known for its ease of access, but they hadn't even bothered to arrange a guide or porters for all their gear. When they heard us ordering dinner with the few words of Nepalese we had managed to pick up along the way, they insisted we aid them in the business of hiring the new team. It was laughable. The climbing permit alone had cost them a small fortune, yet here they were, arguing over a pittance to have these young men bear the brunt of all their shiny equipment, as well as show them the way. It hardly seemed fair.

Wherever we went, we always tried to learn some basic words and phrases of the local language, partly out of respect, and partly to help get ourselves out of sticky situations. Like when no one spoke a word of English, as was the case with these porters. As a fellow foreigner, I was embarrassed for their lack of planning and seeming arrogance.

We ended up spending a second night with their group at the next village. The wife of the group leader was not going to climb. She was going to man the radio at their base camp. But when the morning arrived, she refused to get out of bed, and I awoke to the pathetic sight of her husband sitting on the edge of her bed holding a cup of tea and pleading with her to please get up. She just kept moaning, 'I can't. I can't. I feel sick. It's the food.' I couldn't help but think their little expedition might be seriously doomed.

While I judged the climbers from a distance, my own lack of planning was silently ironic. I, too, had taken off on a wild adventure into the mountains without much forethought. I hadn't fully considered the consequences of what I was doing, walking away from civilisation with a baby in my belly. You could argue that it was irresponsible. But there was also something to be said for a positive mindset. Did things go wrong in our lives because we imagined they might? Did things not go wrong in our lives because we never thought they would? It was an interesting concept, and one that occupied my mind for many hours as I walked.

There wasn't much else to do while walking, other than think. It was hard enough just to keep putting one foot in front of the other on yet another seemingly interminable ascent. As much as we went downhill during the first week, we also went uphill, both for hours at a time. There were plenty of well-placed tea shops and resting platforms, and we took full advantage of them, often stopping for much longer than necessary, or wise. The whole journey from trail head to Everest Base Camp was roughly 150 kilometres. That meant we had to cover about 15 kilometres a day. At the pace we were making, it equated to at least eight hours' walking.

I don't think we made bad time. When I looked at other trekkers, we were almost keeping up. Many of them had porters and guides, and weren't carrying anything other than a day pack. We carried a pack each, so all things considered, we were doing well. I don't think I've ever slept so well as I did on those nights we spent in makeshift lodges in the lower foothills. There was a great sense of camaraderie, not only between the trekkers, but also between the innkeepers and the local porters. Some nights, our accommodation consisted of just one big room, fireplace in the centre, which doubled as the kitchen. The menu featured just one dish - *dal baht* - and it wasn't always great. But there was no choice. I needed the energy for the next day, and to protect me from the chill evening air. More than once I went to sleep with smoke in my eyes, cowering in my sleeping bag to stop them from watering endlessly.

We usually set off at around 7 a.m. each morning, and we were often the first to leave. Many days, breakfast was either the last apple we had in our packs, or non-existent. The people who ran the lodges apparently weren't early risers, at least not early enough to have stoked the coals and cooked breakfast for hungry trekkers. We could have waited around, but with the challenges that lay ahead each day, we chose not to.

I had to ask myself constantly why I was doing this, spending my days climbing hills in dirty, sweat-soaked clothes, and bathing in streams when the opportunity arose. What was it, apart from the amazing scenery, that led me into the mountains? Why insist on pushing myself to the limits of exhaustion? I'd grown up on the coast; beaches and waves were in my blood. Yet, for some reason, I felt quite at home in the Himalaya. I got used to the fact that life was a struggle. Mine was certainly a lot easier than those who lived here. For them, the process of sustaining life was a daily battle - for water, for food, for heating. They had to tend to rice paddies, chickens and buffalo, and higher up it was potatoes and yaks, highly labour-intensive crops. Did they question the meaning of life, or was that purely a luxury of the privileged foreigner? Did we only look for meaning in our lives because we had spare time, money or both?

And what was the meaning of life anyway? Why did we think we might find answers by putting ourselves through this? My Dad once said to me, 'You say that travel is a learning experience, so tell me what you've learnt.'

But it wasn't that simple. Sure, travelling is going places, seeing the world, finding out about other peoples and other cultures, how they live. But it is so much more, more that is not easily communicated verbally. It's not just about the rest of the world. It's also about you - who you are, who you really are; how you cope when things go wrong; how you deal with fear; how you live with less; what makes you happy; what you have to be grateful for.

As it turned out, there was much to be grateful for, not least of which was having the opportunity to come to places like this and walk where not many have. And it was while I was walking that I realised I could live with less, a lot less. But I would have killed for a real, hot shower.

I got that chance in Namche Bazaar, a larger Sherpa village on the doorstep of Everest. At almost 4,000 metres, it was one of two mandatory rest stops on the trail. Avoiding mountain sickness involved acclimatising gradually to the rarefied atmosphere. Walking in from the trail head certainly helped, but it was still necessary to spend two nights in Namche, and another two at the monastery another day's walk to the north. It also meant you could do some washing - of clothes, and yourself.

I can't remember now how much I paid for the luxury of a hot shower, but it wasn't near enough for the work that went into providing it to me. The water had first to be heated over the fire in the kitchen on the top floor of the lodge and then allowed to cool to a temperature less than scalding. It was then poured into a container with a gravity feed to the tiny shed-cum-cubicle on the ground floor, three floors below. I had to keep turning the tap on and off to preserve the tiny amount and still have enough left to remove all traces of soap and shampoo. In between, it was freezing.

It wasn't luxurious by any stretch of the imagination, but the chance to scrape off the ground in dirt that had accumulated under layers of scarcely-removed clothing was pure gold. That was another consequence of coming here. Small things, things we often took for granted or overlooked the value of, became monumental gifts.

The hardest part about being a pregnant trekker was the increasingly frequent, middle of the night bathroom visit. Invariably, the toilets were located outside and far from the lodge, and often a communal arrangement that was simply a shed with a couple of planks above a hole in the ground. In the freezing cold, the accumulated waste sometimes failed to fall to the bottom of the pit, instead forming a dangerous stalagmite-type growth. It was hard to negotiate by torch light, and dangerous if you weren't aware of the lay of the land, so to speak. Just saying.

The trail between Thangboche Monastery and Pheriche would have been easy at a lower altitude, but at over 4,000 metres it was taxing. The cold seeped up through the soles of my shoes and kept my lower legs in a painful, icy state. Walking was the only way to keep the blood flowing. When we reached the village, we hunkered down into our sleeping bags around the tiny, coal brazier and ate everything going.

When we retired, at 7.30 pm, I made the mistake of curling up in a ball inside my sleeping bag, forgetting that it's body heat that keeps the bag warm inside. In the middle of the night I needed to stretch out my legs, but the bottom of the bag was colder than an ice box. Stretched out or curled up, either way was painful. It was a night of fitful sleep, and the coldest yet.

But reaching the edge of the Khumbu glacier and climbing up onto the moraine was reward for all the hardship. Not when I looked down, of course, and I did have to look down. The path from Lobuche across the glacier to Gorakhpur and Base Camp was constantly changing due to the slow, downward crawl of the glacier, and the icebergs which it contained. More than once we had to make a new path for ourselves, since we would have to have been giants to make the leaps over the ever-widening crevasses that stood before us. But when I looked up, the glory of the Himalaya surrounded me on all sides. Massive peaks rode high into the velvety blue sky, forming a breathtaking panorama. I felt tiny, irrelevant, humbled. I was an alien in a beautiful but hostile land. I might have been the only person on the planet.

Gorakshep consisted of a single hut, and if we hadn't been looking for it, we would have missed it. Each night in trekking season, it housed around 16 exhausted and uncomfortable people, lying side by side and end to end. That was the reason we chose to make Lobuche our base, and the trek to Base Camp and Kala Pattar a day trip. It was only a two-hour walk each way, though it felt like much more in the thin air. The food at our lodge in Lobuche was also to die for, the best I'd had on the entire trek. *Didi's* Sherpa stew was almost a good enough reason to have come all this way. Almost.

There's a lot to be said for pilgrimage, and for me, that's what this trek had become. I was so proud of myself. I had set myself a goal and a challenge, and I had risen to the occasion, even with a baby on board. I had walked for weeks to get to a place few people would ever see for themselves, a place so remote that the world I knew really ceased to exist. I had found time in the silence to understand that the answers I was seeking were not here, or anywhere else for that matter. They had been within me all along. I just didn't know it until I came here and did this. So, that is why I came.

NINETEEN

The Trouble with Lukla

GETTING IN TO THE EVEREST REGION OF NEPAL by walking for several weeks for eight to ten hours a day was one thing. Getting out again was quite another. Some opted to walk both ways, savouring the long days in the middle hills and the quaint little tea houses and lodges. We decided to go with the flight out of Lukla, about three days' walk down from base camp.

Lukla was always crowded in trekking season. A lot of people flew both ways to save time. They missed out on a lot of breathtaking scenery and interaction with the locals. Plus, it was much easier to acclimatise if you walked all the way. We met a couple of people going up who told us they had five days to get to base camp. Right. Considering it was necessary to stay two nights at two different altitudes, they were setting themselves up for failure. And we met them a few days later, descending because the symptoms of altitude sickness had set in. Surprise, surprise.

The trouble with Lukla was all to do with its geography. Perched on the edge of the Dudh Khosi valley about 500 metres above the river bed, the town was wedged in between two snow-capped mountain ridges. It was on the edge of a natural wind tunnel. And when the wind got up, the daily flights from Kathmandu didn't happen. That often led to a lot of trekkers stranded in the village, all clamouring to get out.

The day we arrived, severe weather had caused the cancellation of all flights for the last three days. The foreigners were all a bit antsy. On top of this, we hadn't pre-purchased our tickets before we left Kathmandu. It was too hard to predict the actual day we would want to fly. Consequently, we were the lowest of the low in the pecking order.

We awoke the next morning to find clear blue skies and no wind. It was looking good for at least a couple of flights. But by 7 a.m., the man at the check-in counter was thronged by tourists and locals alike, all waving tickets in his face and demanding to be put on a flight. But he had seen it all before. He didn't care who had tickets and who didn't. He didn't even know whether there would be any flights at all until the first plane landed. He was unmoved by the pleas from the crowd. The only rule he cared to enforce was the one that permitted foreigners to leave first. No locals on the first two flights. If there were that many.

Since porters and guides accompanied many of the tourists, they were keen to get them onto the same flight out. But some were quick to abandon them when it came to the crunch. An elderly Swiss gentleman stubbornly pointed out that his porter also held a valid ticket.

'First flight, foreigners only,' the clerk said. 'You want to fly or not?' Reluctantly, he admitted that he did.

Suddenly, our tickets were snatched from my hand and rubber stamped for a flight. 'You have luggage? Bring it now!' the clerk barked in my general direction. A young woman standing beside me spoke up, unable to bear the injustice of us going first.

'Which flight are you on?' She wasn't happy. I had no idea. I shrugged. I was happy to be on any flight.

'That's not fair. We were here before her. We were here yesterday. We're on the list.' She stabbed at the piece of paper that lay on the desk. The clerk sighed, slapped our tickets back on the counter and checked her in instead. She was travelling with her father and a Nepalese porter.

'First flight, foreigners only.'

'Fine. Just the two of us, then,' she replied without the slightest hesitation. Her porter glanced my way and shrugged, giving me a toothy smile. He looked happy to finally be rid of her.

Next to get allocated a flight was a large group of Japanese. We were demoted again, along with all the Nepalese, to the third of nine flights that were expected to arrive shortly. Did it matter which one we were on? The airport hall soon cleared and everyone went to wait by the fence for the sound of propellers to drift up the valley. It wasn't a long wait.

In the 1980s, the runway at Lukla was still gravel, and strewn with boulders. Inbound flights had to fly up the narrow valley and perform a 90-degree right hand turn at the last minute to make it onto the runway, which sloped upwards towards the terminal building. Just short of the high end, the plane wheeled around on the spot and came to a sudden stop in a cloud of dust. The undercarriage opened and more luggage than the plane seemed capable of carrying was thrown out. It was replaced with the outgoing pile. A handful of passengers boarded, and it was gone again, leaving behind several backpacks that hadn't made the cut.

The Japanese passengers were invited to climb over the fence to await the arrival of the second flight, which was followed very closely by the third, and a government helicopter. Because they were already on the runway, they were blasted with dust as the three flying machines stopped at their feet. The helicopter quickly took off again, finding even more dirt to spray over the gaggle of waiting passengers.

Suddenly, our flight was called and motioned to board, ahead of the Japanese. We squeezed between them and the fence to get to the plane. Our bags were thrown in behind us and the door slammed shut. Completely unexpectedly, a tall, thin woman in an impeccably folded sari offered me a tray of candies and cotton wool. She seemed oblivious to the fact that I was struggling with my seat, which had folded in half behind me. Without making any move to assist me, she moved to rear of the cabin, fastened her own seat belt, and stared off into the distance.

My seat was directly behind the cockpit, which had neither door nor curtain to separate it from the cabin. Since there were no allocated seats, I had chosen the front row in the hope of getting a bird's eye view of the trails we had just spent several weeks labouring up and down. As we sat at the top of the runway, I began to regret my decision. I also began to feel sick.

I watched in horror as the two pilots throttled the little plane up to full power. They had both feet on the brakes, legs at full stretch. When they finally released them, we were catapulted down the slope, bouncing over the uneven surface. And random boulders.

I knew the runway ended in a huge cliff, and we didn't get off the ground until the very last minute. Directly in front of us, smack bang in our path, was a mountain. To the right was Everest, which I had to crouch to see out the window. It felt like we were free-falling. We probably were for several seconds, until the plane suddenly made a 90-degree turn to the left. The gusts of wind grew ever stronger, buffeting the plane around like some tiny feather. It was so noisy. At last, the reason for the tray of cotton wool was revealed. I had wondered. Now I thought it might be to drown out the sound of the plane breaking into two or more pieces as the fuselage twisted and writhed.

From my bird's eye view seat, all I could see were the white knuckles of the pilots wrestling with the controls. As we neared Lamjura Pass, we began to ride the pockets of air like a roller coaster. When I was brave enough to look out the window, I subconsciously chanted the names of villages we had spent weeks walking through, and which now disappeared beneath us in just minutes. I felt both elated and disappointed, watching the terraced mountains below. So glad for all that I had achieved, despite the hardships of the past few weeks. And so sad that it would soon be over. There's something remarkable that comes with personal triumph, no matter how small it may be in the scheme of things - a sense of fulfilment and confidence; the belief that anything is possible if you put effort to it. And I had found it in the mountains of my beloved Nepal.

A young Sherpa boy seated behind me suddenly flung his arms around my seat. And me. I turned and smiled at him as I tried to loosen his grip. He laughed, almost hysterically, which was weird because I couldn't hear him over the noise.

I only started to relax when the huge white dome of the Bodhinath stupa came into view, its colourful prayer flags hailing our return to the Kathmandu Valley. We were going to make it.

We landed perfectly, as if we had just floated in on the breeze.

After mingling momentarily on the tarmac with the passengers for a departing international flight, we were scooped up by a waiting taxi and ferried back into the bustle and clamour of the city's early morning. But I silently appreciated the sealed cocoon that preserved, for just a little longer, the tranquillity that comes only from the high Himalayan foot paths.

TWENTY

Backpackers Phone Home

ONE OF THE THINGS WE ALWAYS LOOKED FORWARD TO out on the road was contact with 'home'. But there were no smart phones or tablets with which to capture the moment, or the latest interesting meal. No selfies with awesome backgrounds and new-found friends, even nothing to keep the lines of communication open. The Internet had been invented, but nobody knew about it. And it definitely wasn't available for public use. Hell, back in those days, computers were giant machines housed in their own air-conditioned buildings, and accessing them meant colouring in little lines on pre-printed pieces of yellow cardboard. And if you coloured outside the lines, the whole program would crash. Communication was still in the dark ages.

I couldn't count the number of times I had wished for some of my friends to be with us, sharing the experiences - relaxing over coffee, cake, and hash fumes in the cafes of Kathmandu. Or lounging around on the parapets of temples in Bagan. Or playing cards and chatting late into the night on the trekking paths of the Himalaya.

So, it wasn't surprising that whenever we arrived in a new, sizable city, a visit to the local post office was high on the agenda. Letters from home, or even better, care packages full of impossible-to get goodies, were highly prized and much appreciated. After gathering our stash of mail from Poste Restante, we would hightail it to the nearest cafe to read and re-read all the latest news from 'the old country'.

But every now and then, we just needed to hear a familiar voice. And that meant a trip to the local telephone office.

After six weeks in the mountains, isolated from everyone and everything known to us, a phone call home was in order. Not just for us, but for the sakes of those on the other end of the phone. In Kathmandu, it was an exercise that required much preparation and planning. Food, water, blankets, something comfortable to sit on, and wheelbarrows of the local currency were prerequisites. Why? Because it usually took more than three freaking hours to get through. Sometimes, depending on the local weather conditions in Timbuktu, you might not get through at all. Even after you had waited three hours already.

The process was tedious. On arrival, the first thing you noticed was the crowd; at least 20 others waiting in line ahead of you. And not much space left to sit, or even stand. A clerk at the main desk, surrounded by a sea of paperwork and paperweights, eventually found it within herself to provide you with the application form. You filled this out by hand, in triplicate, with carbon paper between each copy - name, local address, passport number, country you wished to call, area code, phone number, name of person you wished to speak to, and approximately how long you intended to converse. Then you moved aside, and waited. And waited. And watched everyone else enter the little booth. Watched them re-emerge. And leave. And then you waited some more.

After several hours of rinse and repeat most of the above steps, your name would be called. Inside the individual booths was a telephone, one of the old-fashioned ones that had a receiver section and a black box with silver buttons - Button A and Button B. When the phone made a vaguely familiar ringing sound, you picked up the receiver. And waited. Sometimes there would be the sound of interference, and sometimes, the sound of silence. Eventually, a barely-intelligible voice with an impossibly thick accent would ask you which country you were calling. What the? Then, guess what? You waited some more!

If you were lucky, and the telecommunications gods were on your side, and if the wind was blowing from the west while you stood on one leg, then maybe, just maybe, you would get to hear the voice of a loved one. Sometimes you got to determine the length of the call. And sometimes it just dropped out. All that was left to do was to pay for the privilege of wasting most of your afternoon or evening. In Nepal, it cost hundreds of rupees. So, no surprise it was not something we did every day, or even every week. We just carried on waiting on snail mail, which was also unreliable, but not destined to drop out after a few minutes.

Those we had left at home probably never understood how we treasured their letters. They were a sparse reminder that we still belonged somewhere in the world, even if no one knew exactly where we were. Even if we didn't feel as connected as we once were. The longer we were away, the more those feelings of independence grew. And now, with a baby to think about, our choices had become all the more significant. We would return for the birth. That was the obvious choice. But everything would be different. We were different. Even if not much had changed for anyone else.

TWENTY-ONE

High Tea in the Hill Station

WE DIDN'T STAY MUCH LONGER IN NEPAL after the Everest trek. After spending several months, on and off, in the Kingdom, we needed a new perspective from which to view life. The trek to Everest Base Camp had allowed me time for a deep, introspective look at my life and the future with a new baby in it. Though the birth was still more than six months away, I felt the need to start making some plans beyond which country to visit next.

Originally, we had intended to fly from Kathmandu to Colombo, Sri Lanka, when we were done poking around Nepal. But civil war broke out there around the same time, and put paid to those plans. We had to get back to Bangkok to cash in the tickets we had purchased previously from one of the many bucket shops. So, we made our next move in that direction. East.

The first major distraction was Darjeeling, a hill station popular with the Raj in the Indian state of West Bengal. And home of the famous Darjeeling tea plantations. The bus that conveyed us from Kathmandu to the eastern border with India was more comfortable than the usual transport out of the Valley. That was a good thing since it was going to be a ten-hour overnight journey. The padded, reclining seats were an unexpected luxury, even if they were covered in a shiny vinyl that made them hot and sticky.

Somewhere along the way, on the vast, flat expanse of the *terai*, we got to witness another glorious Indian sunrise. The dust in the air made the burnt red globe appear massive on the eastern horizon. The heavily-tinted windows of the bus removed any vestige of glare. It made my skin tingle, and I was transported back to my first day in India, when I had also watched the sun rise from the window of a bus. For some reason, I always felt closest to India at sunrise, more willing to overlook its faults.

The border officials on this side of the country seemed much more relaxed than the others we had encountered. It may have been because this entry and exit point was less popular and saw far fewer travellers than the others. Even the Indians gave us no cause to complain as we crossed over in the early morning mist. Until we were loaded onto a waiting bus headed for Siliguri. Suddenly, we were reminded that we were back in India, land of crowds, confusion, discomfort, and rising tempers. Thankfully, it was only a 40-minute trip.

The easiest way to get from Siliguri to Darjeeling was by shared taxi. Unfortunately, we had to share our taxi, an ageing Hindustan Ambassador, with six others - the driver, three random locals, a German pearl diver, and an American Jesuit priest who couldn't bring himself to be quiet. He regaled us with tales of his thirty years in India for the entire journey, which wouldn't have been so bad had it been the slightest bit interesting. The Ambassador may have been big, but it was still not big enough for that many people - eight altogether. Four in the front and four in the back. It was another uncomfortable three hours on a switch backing road up the mountains.

But the township of Darjeeling was worth the trouble. Laced over the side of a western-facing ridge, all locations in the town provided clear and uninterrupted views of Kanchenjunga, the third highest mountain in the world, and its surrounding ranges. Steep sets of stone stairs connected the narrow streets, and walking anywhere in town required climbing them, both up and down.

We found a quaint little lodge without any fuss, and promptly booked a hot shower. That translated to a bucket of slightly warmer than tepid water, which we were meant to tip over our stripped-down bodies. The temperature of the air at 2,000 metres was not conducive to such a task, even in mid-afternoon, so I decided to make do with a quick, very quick, top and tail. With all the layers of clothing I was wearing, no one was going to notice, apart from me.

The township proper had a tinge of faded Raj about it. The vestiges of the old British Empire were everywhere. The landmark cafe, The Glenary, occupied prime position for viewing the distant mountain ranges. It also served up the best high tea outside London. So, it quickly became our first choice for breakfast, lunch and afternoon tea.

After a fine rendition of eggs on toast, we headed off to find the right office from which to post a parcel. Indian parcels had to be wrapped in calico sewn together with string. For a small fee, a little old man with a big-eyed needle would do it for you, infinitely better than trying to find all the bits and pieces required by yourself. In Darjeeling, finding such a little old man turned out to be a relatively easy task, and the posting was completed quickly and painlessly.

A helpful lady at the local Tourist Office marked out a circular walk on our map that took us around the edge of the city, taking in the Tibetan Refugee Camp and North Point. It was a peaceful, six-kilometre loop that offered expansive views of the stunning Kanchenjunga range and the endless tea plantations. I never tired of the views of the Himalaya, distant as they were. They were always there, in the back of my mind, if not visible. They were the reason I came and the reason I stayed. And one day, they would be one of the best reasons I could find to return. They would always have my heart.

Not far above the town was the famous vantage point of Tiger Hill. Rumour had it that a beautiful lodge sat atop the ridge, with rooms that contained the most comfortable beds in the whole of India. And an open fireplace to boot. The thought of it was enticing. We left our luggage at the Tourist Office after breakfast the next day, and climbed the trail up to the lodge. As described in our guide book, it was typically British in design, and our two-dollar room was the size of a ball room. It also included dinner, which was a communal event, taken with all the other guests at a massive wooden dining table and served by men in white uniforms. So special.

We were woken at 5 a.m. the next morning so that we could make the short walk to the peak in time for sunrise. It was still dark, the rising sun just a pinkish glow on the eastern horizon. It was hard to climb out of a warm bed in the brisk mountain morning, but the views that were waiting for us at the Observatory would be the highlight of our visit. Unfortunately, crowds of locals in taxis also had the same idea, and on the tiny, wooden viewing platform, we mingled cheek to cheek. It appeared that every man, woman and child had their own camera, and all of them wanted to capture the perfect sunrise photo, with or without themselves in it. But most of the resulting pictures were probably marred by the backs of a hundred heads. For those without cameras, a few old men were selling postcards of the view. Nobody wanted them.

When the sun finally rose above the dust and haze that covered West Bengal and Bangladesh, Kanchenjunga danced to her tune, turning first crimson, then pale pink, then brilliant yellow. It was magic in action.

TWENTY-TWO

Toy Trains and UFOs

AFTER ONE FINAL BREAKFAST AT THE GLENARY, we said goodbye to the peaceful atmosphere of the hill station and returned to the intensity of the Indian plains. The Toy Train was an appropriate way to get back there, taking its sweet time to trundle down the steep, switch backing track to Siliguri in true 'I think I can' style. Though it was a good eight-hour trip on hard seats, the breathtaking scenery and the antics of the young boys who chased our carriage and played chicken with the slow-moving engine more than compensated. We could have done without the light covering of smoke and ash from the engine blowing in through the open windows. But hey, it was all part of the splendid experience. As we neared our changeover station, New Jalpaiguri, a misty haze covered the plains, making for another stunning sunset experience.

I sat quietly, staring out the window into the settling darkness for what seemed like ages. I realised I was sad to be leaving India, a thought that made me wonder if I had finally lost my mind. The subcontinent had cajoled me, confounded me, annoyed me, frustrated me, and at times, made me wish it all to hell. But above all, it had seduced me into believing in the endless possibilities life had to offer. We could make of it what we would, but it all came down to opportunities and choices. Granted, some of us had more to choose from than others merely by our birthright. We all had our own crosses to bear; and yes, some were heavy.

A flash of light in the sky just outside the window suddenly broke my reverie. As I watched, three coloured lights, red, green and yellow, flipped around, changed shape and moved in weird and unexpected trajectories. I tried to make sense of the shapes they formed, but it was illogical. Others on the train were watching, too. We stared at each other blankly, completely at a loss to explain what we were seeing. The lights stayed with us, travelling up and down the length of the moving train for at least fifteen minutes, long enough for us all to realise we were not imagining things.

Then, just as suddenly as they had appeared, they were gone. No camera or video or smart phone had recorded the event. There was no evidence that it had even happened. For the rest of the trip, the carriage was eerily quiet apart from the noise of the steam engine chugging away.

We changed trains in New Jalpaiguri for the Siliguri Express to Calcutta. It was kind of a misnomer that any train Indian train should be called an express. They were always delayed for one reason or another - cows on the tracks, people on the tracks, vehicles stuck on the tracks, somewhere the driver wanted to stop for a visit or a quick *puja* (worship). The reasons were as endless as the journeys often seemed.

There was a too-long conversation with an officious clerk at the Foreigners' Registration Office inside the station about where we had come from. Was it so unusual to have gotten off the Toy Train from Darjeeling? Were we the only ones to have ever made the trip? You could be forgiven for thinking that we had broken some unwritten holy law, so intense was his questioning.

The curries in the station restaurant were as bad as every other railway station dinner. Forgettable. But the train to Calcutta pulled away from the platform before I'd finished even one more chapter of

James Clavell's *Shogun*, a monstrous tome that had gotten me through many a tedious train and bus trip over the last couple of months. Travelling in India was perfect for getting a bit of light reading done. I had already waded through the Salman Rushdie classics, *Freedom at Midnight* and *Midnight's Children*, and Dominique Lapierre's *City of Joy*, all highly recommended even if you aren't trying to while away time on an endless train trip.

Because of the heat, it was a fitful night of sleep on the Siliguri Express. And it was cut woefully short by a guy who seemed to think that everyone in the carriage needed to wake up at 5 a.m. and buy one of his combs. Yes, that's right. Combs. He started hawking his wares right beside my ear as I slept on an upper tier berth, above the window where all the hot air stagnated. He held his sample comb aloft, waved it through his own oily black mop, presumably to show how it worked, all the while yelling at the top of his voice to make sure that no one remained asleep. If I could have understood a word he was saying, I would surely have realised that this comb was what I had been waiting for my entire life.

Several people yelled at him, obviously to shut the hell up. But it had no effect. From my vantage point, right behind his head, I could easily have whacked him, and I started looking around for that doorstop of a novel I was reading. Just then, the *chai wallahs* appeared and started making their way through the carriage. Since I was already wide awake, a cup of tea was probably the more sensible option. That was one thing about an Indian train. You could always get a cup of hot tea.

And a comb.

TWENTY-THREE

Kolkata

I'VE ALWAYS THOUGHT that if Kolkata, or Calcutta as I knew it, had been the first place I had visited in India, I probably would have left immediately and never gone back. It was a tough gig, whichever way you looked at it. Though no more crowded than any other large Indian city, the poverty was overwhelming. Nowhere else in the country had I seen such badly mutilated beggars - people with no arms, no legs, no hands. A man wriggled down the street on his hands and knees, the latter shielded from the pavement by pieces of rubber cut from old tyre tubes. Whole families lived on the footpaths. Mothers washed their children and their clothes on the streets, right between the tram tracks. There were stories that parents purposely mutilated their children, broke their arms or legs, just so they could command pity as beggars. It was a cruel world, full of unimaginable tragedy. Early in the mornings, the air was almost unbreathable and visibility was extremely low. It usually cleared a little by late morning, if only to prove the sky was still blue.

We spent Christmas 1983 in Calcutta. Who would have thought. We dressed up a wonky bedside table with a colourful cloth and stood a bunch of red roses and white chrysanthemums in a yogurt pot as a makeshift Christmas tree. Other than that, we never would have known it was Christmas. And that was odd. Christmas had traditionally been a time to spend with family. And this one, only the second in our young married life, was so much farther from that than just a few thousand miles. We did try to make a phone call home, but, as in Nepal, the line was long and the wait interminable, and after three hot, sweaty hours, we still couldn't get through.

Our last days in India were mostly spent resting, far from the crowds in our fan-cooled hotel room. So long in India had worn me down, blurred my senses with its myriad problems. And Calcutta didn't help. It wasn't a poetic ending to the experience. Everybody, it seemed, wanted something. And they were desperate to get it, one way or another. Nowhere was this more evident than in Calcutta, where life was cheap and death an everyday event. Something that settled like dust, unnoticed.

Leaving India for the bureaucracy of Burma was almost like going on holiday. In many ways, it was a relief. We had met many different people from many different places. Some of them loved India; others hated it. The ones who hated it had worked that out quickly, and hadn't stayed long. But that was partly the problem. You had to get past the dirt, the heat, the filth, the hassles and the poverty. And that took time. India wasn't a country you could visit for a couple of weeks and expect to enjoy. Full appreciation of its uniqueness required much longer.

After a couple of months, it had gotten to me in undeniable ways. It had made me confront my own norms, challenged the way I viewed the world. It made me realise, over and over, how easy life was for us at home. Back in Australia, things usually went according to plan. Usually. We could pick up a phone and book a taxi, and it would turn up at the appointed time. The driver would flick on his meter without argument, and take us exactly where we asked to go. Not so here. We had to fight to get a taxi, fight over whether or not the meter was turned on, or argue about the price if it wasn't. Hell, we even had to argue about our destination, otherwise the driver was likely to take us somewhere where he would get a commission just for dropping us off. Nothing was easy. Everything was a drama. Some days it felt like the whole world was out to get me, to rip me off. And that pissed me off.

But at the same time, I was embarrassed by my reaction to these difficulties. I was like a little kid. If things went against me, I got the shits. I complained. I got angry with everyone else for making my life a misery. I laid blame with reckless abandon. But you know what? I put myself there. I chose to go there, to travel, to experience a different side of life; to learn new things and try to see life from someone else's point of view. Why on earth was I so upset? India created an intense internal struggle for me, a love-hate relationship. Parts of it were breathtakingly beautiful. Parts of it were ugly as sin. But at the end of the day, it was all part of the same living tapestry, more than the sum of its parts. I just had to learn to appreciate the whole, even if the parts didn't make any sense on their own.

TWENTY-FOUR

Take me to the Black Market

WE ARRIVED IN BURMA LATE ONE AFTERNOON, off the flight from Calcutta, bottle of Johnny Walker Red Label and carton of 555 cigarettes at our sides. You might be wondering why on earth I would mention that, but believe me, there was a twisted logic behind the duty-frees. And the explanation will probably surprise you.

In 1983, Burmese visas were issued for seven days only. No exceptions. Even if your outgoing flight was cancelled, as we discovered on our second visit. But I digress.

After the immigration officials had finished filling up all the available space on several pages of our passports, we were handed a piece of paper with the title, Currency Exchange Document, and allowed to pass through the doors into Burma, as the country was called before they changed it to Myanmar.

There was a long queue at the currency exchange counter, but it was necessary to get in it so that we could get some money for our taxi into the city. While we waited, we met the people standing in front of and behind us, as you do when you're standing in an endless, slow-moving line, sweating like the proverbial and complaining about getting dicked around by bureaucracy. Sally was a fellow Australian who started every sentence with the words, 'When I was in Siri Lanka...'

and, no, that is not a typo. That's how she pronounced the name. In the coming days it was going to drive us right up the wall.

Stefan was Scandinavian and strongly resembled the Viking stereotype. Once we had gotten our cash and had our Currency Exchange Documents duly stamped, Stefan looked in the direction of the bank of waiting taxis and announced, 'Take me to the Black Market.' He wasn't kidding.

The funny thing about seven days in Burma in the early 80s had everything to do with the exchange rate for the *kyat* (pronounced chut), the local currency. Burmese officials had control over the exchange rate, and bringing *kyat* in and taking it out of the country was illegal. The exchange rate was also set at the ridiculously low level of six to the US dollar, a rate that could be bettered by more than five times on the streets. If you were cluey. And careful.

The duty frees we were clutching on arrival were the keys to a very cheap tour of an already cheap country. There was no substitute for the brand of whisky and cigarettes. It was Johnny Walker Red Label and 555 cigarettes they wanted, and nothing else. These two items, purchased for approximately $15 US at the airport in Calcutta, were going to fetch double that at the black-market exchange rate, and more than $100 at the official rate. With two of us participating in the jollies, that money would be enough to see us make the Rangoon-Bagan-Mandalay loop, so popular with just about everyone who entered the country, without changing any more money. Officially.

Because of the official attempt to manipulate the exchange rate in this way, there was a raging black market for US dollars. The Currency Exchange Document was meant to exercise some control over what happened to the coveted tourist dollars. But it was less than useless. Every transaction we made was supposed to be recorded, including how much was spent, and the current balance we were holding in both US dollars and *kyat*. Only the larger hotels and airlines showed any interest whatsoever in filling it out. Local restaurants, taxis, trains, street stalls - none of them even knew what it was. Can you imagine trying to convince a city bus driver in any city to fill out such a form as you boarded their bus? In my experience, bus drivers all over the world had roughly the same temperament - frazzled, frustrated and impatient. And anyway, if you paid in US dollars, you still got your change in *kyat*, no matter what.

We exited the smallish arrivals hall into the faces of a hundred young men posing as taxi drivers. Stefan repeated his desire to be taken to the Black Market. A couple of young kids herded us towards their car, a bottle green and white Zephyr that looked like it had been driving around since the 1950s, and we got in. Aside from the colour, its most notable feature was several gaping holes in the floor, through which the road was clearly visible. Rust had clearly taken hold some time ago, and been ignored.

The boys were friendly, which kind of made up for the fact that the car had no floor. They prattled on in passable English, suggesting all kinds of tourist destinations that they could help us navigate. But mostly they just tried to buy our duty frees. They successfully got both of ours at an equivalent exchange rate of about 23 *kyat* to the dollar, which was going to prove to be enough for the whole week in country. I wasn't sure what to do with that Currency Exchange Document now.

Stefan managed to keep hold of his duty-frees until we got to our hotel. He was rewarded for that by an even better exchange rate. Most people were divested of their goodies either in the airport hall or in the taxi to the city. If you managed to get them all the way to Mandalay, the rates were phenomenal. But by then, the need for *kyat* had also seriously diminished.

So, we had seven days to spend in Burma - see as much as you can, don't stop too long, don't pass go, don't collect $200. Or too many *kyat*. We pretty much travelled everywhere with the people who had arrived on the same day. There was so much to see and so little time to do it. Everyone we met and discussed travel plans with started their sentences with, 'If I have time...' It seemed that everything was a must-see or not-to-be-missed attraction. There was nothing for it but to get on the loop - Rangoon, Bagan, Mandalay and back.

TWENTY-FIVE

On the

Burma in 7 Days Loop

AT THE TOP OF EVERYONE'S LIST of places to see was Pagan, or Bagan as they call it now. It was a long way from Rangoon, requiring an overnight train trip to Thazi, an early morning bus ride to Nyaung-oo, and several journeys on transport ranging from jeep to horse and cart to finally reach our destination. The last seven kilometres from Nyaung-oo delivered us to the village across the vast Irrawaddy flood plain, littered with a mind-boggling number of temples and stupas. They rose out of the landscape in every direction. In the late afternoon sun, they were painted in hues of pink and gold. Stunning.

We were travelling with Sally and Stefan, and all the strangers we hadn't met at the airport on our arrival. We did come to recognise their faces, as we passed them on the tourist trail with monotonous regularity. To get around the beautiful pagodas, we hired Min and his horse-drawn cart for the day. Ten temples and the Nyaung-oo markets was probably a bit ambitious. Each stop meant another climb on dark, narrow stone staircases that reeked of bat guano. It would have been exhausting even if I hadn't been five months' pregnant at the time. Still, once I reached the towering parapets, I felt a great sense of peace as I looked out over the broad, flat river plain.

It would have been easy to spend the whole officially-sanctioned week exploring Pagan, but bureaucracy would not allow it. After just a couple of nights, we were on another early morning jeep with about 20 others, headed for Mandalay. There was just enough time to visit Mandalay Hill, the huge local markets and the famous Nylon Ice Cream Bar, a rare treat on the Asian highways, in our allotted 24-hour stay.

We got around Mandalay on cute little bicycle rickshaws, one at a time, each passenger facing backwards behind the driver. The only downside of the trip was having to haggle over a reasonable price. It took half an hour, which was almost as long as the entire journey. Even though we had all had something less than an hour's sleep, we had to get all our sightseeing and ticket-buying done in one day, because the following day, we would be back on the night express to Rangoon. It was rather a shame, because Mandalay looked worthy of a much longer visit.

By the time we arrived back in the capital, I was so tired I could no longer think. Which probably explains why, on day six of our week-long adventure, I bought a cane baby cradle at the city markets. I didn't even consider how we might travel with it from here on out, or what a hassle that would turn out to be. The only way to get it on the plane was to secure one of our backpacks inside it. It certainly raised a few eyebrows at the seven or so airports we passed through post purchase. I found myself answering the same question everywhere it appeared: 'Where baby?' Well, given the size of my belly by now, I did think that might have been obvious.

We made one last visit to the Diplomatic Store in Rangoon to pick up some souvenirs. Strangely though, the most prominent items on the shelves were... Johnny Walker Red Label whisky and cartons of 555 cigarettes, all bearing the same stickers. In small print, they all announced, 'Purchased in Singapore (or Bangkok, or Calcutta), Duty Not Paid.' I wonder how they got there.

I hadn't thought much about my Currency Exchange form over the last week. It hadn't been needed. But the night before we left Burma, we realised that we would have to hand it in on our departure the next day. The whirlwind tour had been hectic, and filled with local sightseeing on various forms of transport. There had been little time for currency forms, nor even any need to change money. The money we had secured in the taxi from the airport into Rangoon had been more than enough to see us through a whole week. Hence, the final night's splurge on dinner at Rangoon's poshest hotel.

Always the enterprising travellers, we all decided that instead of bodgying up our forms with fake transactions, we'd simply use them as place mats underneath our very messy chicken curry dinners. It didn't take too long before the forms, originally filled out in fountain pen, now looked more like watercolour sketch works. Let's see what the customs and immigration officers would make of this.

As I stood patiently in line waiting to get approval to leave this beautiful country, I fingered the form I had made such a mess of and wondered if indeed I would get to leave. When asked, I handed it over and waited for the final decision.

'This is an official government document,' the officer barked at me. He took it gingerly between his thumb and index finger as if it was toxic, and discarded it in the nearest bin without a second glance. What did draw a second glance however, were the cassette tapes he discovered as he checked my hand luggage.

'English cassettes?' he asked.

'Yes,' I replied.

'How much?' *Kyat* were not going to be much use to me on the remainder of our trip, from airport lounge across the tarmac to the plane. Politely, I declined. He seemed genuinely disappointed, but he let me leave the country despite my currency form.

Despite the whirlwind that was Burma all those years ago, I still remember the kindness and sincerity of the Burmese people. The strict visa regulations meant that the people had remained unspoilt by a massive influx of tourists and western influence. Everywhere we went, they wanted to help, to chat, to learn English and about where we were from, and what it was like outside their own country, for they rarely travelled themselves.

The rules have been changed, along with the place names, since we were there. And I'm sure that has also brought changes in the people. For good or bad, I can't say unless I go back. But as I've come to understand, sometimes that is the wrong decision.

TWENTY-SIX

What the FEC!

BACK IN 1984, CHINA WAS THE GREAT UNKNOWN. One could argue that it still is today. Individual travel permits had finally become a reality, although still steeped in bureaucracy. Just getting one in Hong Kong was an adventure. Taking a train from Hung Hom Station was a relatively simple task, even if you did have to detrain and pass through Chinese customs at the border city of Shenzhen. In just a few hours, you could be in Guangzhou. From there on in, it was all trouble. And all in Chinese.

There was nothing easy about travelling around China, at least there wasn't back in the early 80s. The China International Travel Service (CITS for short) had only been granting individual travel permits for a few months when we applied for ours in Hong Kong. It was the easiest place on the planet to get them. For some strange reason, embassies in different countries had different rules for granting visas. In some places, it was impossible to get a visa in the first place, and in others, the conditions attached to them were seriously limiting. Sometimes the cost of the visa even depended on your nationality. If your country was out of favour with the ruling party of the country you wanted to visit, you could forget even getting a foot in the door. But I digress.

Individual travel, on the other hand, was made more difficult by the fact that there were many places you weren't allowed to go without yet another document - the Alien Travel Permit. You were supposed to know in advance where you wanted to go, which cities you planned to visit. It was confronting for two travellers who rarely decided such minor details in advance. These documents were only issued once inside the country. So we had some extra time to decide. We also had to find the place first.

We had heard that the best places to sleep cheap in China were the hotel dormitories. Even the more expensive hotels had one apparently, and the word was that they were clean, warm and relatively empty all around the country. They were frequented by foreign students living in China and travellers in the know.

At the front desk of the Liuhua Hotel, just across the massive concourse and car park of the railway station, we learnt our first Chinese phrase – *meiyou* (pronounced may-oo) meaning 'no have!' *Meiyou* was tied in closely with the Game of Flat Denial, which we also learnt that night. Basically, the longer and louder you said *meiyou*, the more chance you had of convincing the other party. In fact, it was inevitable.

The night we arrived, the dormitory at the Liuhua was *meiyou*. And when we persisted with our request, it became full, too. Naive and frustrated, we lost the game. Standing in line behind us at the reservation desk, an English-speaking Chinese man had witnessed the whole fiasco. Henry introduced himself and suggested that we follow him to another hotel nearby. But the next hotel refused to accept non-Chinese at all. Not only no have, but no want.

Henry very kindly offered to share a more expensive room with us back at the Liuhua. There were few options at that point so, reluctantly, we agreed.

Luckily Henry was not an axe murderer, and we spent the evening listening to him plan our itinerary around China. He was on business from Hong Kong, clearly used to being organised and not at all comfortable with the no-plan, go-with-the-flow mentality of the lowly backpacker scene. In the end, I think he felt sorry for us and, embarrassingly, paid for almost everything. When he checked out the next morning, he saw us on our way to the train station to purchase two tickets to Shanghai, the first stop on our China-according-to-Henry travel plan.

But we didn't check out. We had to have time to plan our own trip around China. Perhaps there were even things of interest in Guangzhou itself. And we had to have another go at getting a spot in the dorm. Our western egos demanded it. Miraculously, the dorms had emptied, and we were granted access. It seemed too easy in the light of day, but we gratefully accepted our fate.

'Third floor. Men and women separate. FEC only. Ten each.' The young girl at the desk, the same one who had screamed *meiyou* in our faces last night, now seemed to speak quite good English. She didn't seem to care that we recognised her as the beastly dormitory gatekeeper from hell. So, we spent another night in Guangzhou. And had some time to look around.

Just as in Burma, there was something of a black market for money in China. Tourists were issued with a completely different currency to the locals, known as FEC - Foreign Exchange Currency. The locals got to use the regular currency - *Renminbi*. Foreign devils were not supposed to use it, or even have it in their possession. But since we were the only ones who possessed FEC, it was inevitable that whenever we spent it, we got our change in *Renminbi*. It wasn't well thought out. Plus, there were places where this FEC money had never been seen, so it just wasn't accepted.

One way or another, we had to get hold of our own stash of *Renminbi*. The word on the backpacker grapevine was that there were quite a few willing 'exchange facilitators' running clandestine operations in the backstreets just around the corner from the Liuhua. And they were surprisingly easy to find, considering this activity was highly illegal. Business was conducted right on the street, in a way that made you feel like you were on the set of a bad spy movie.

Nevertheless, we found said facilitator quickly, told her how much we wanted to change, then waited as instructed. She disappeared for a few minutes, then returned with the appropriate amount of local cash, and we furtively handed over our FEC. It turned out to be the easiest transaction of all our dealings in China.

We also needed an Alien Travel Permit to go pretty much anywhere else in China, except perhaps Shanghai or Beijing. Some places, like Tibet and the far western provinces, were impossible to access from the large and powerful cities, where bureaucracy reigned supreme. Their sordid goal was apparently to protect the rest of China from a foreign invasion. Further west, where many failed to reach, the outposts were more moderate, and more inclined to acquiesce to the whim of a persistent foreign devil. The reach of power obviously didn't cross the vast distances with speed. And back in those days, communication was quite literally at a snail's pace.

When we found the local Office of Public Security, we had our Alien Travel Permits stamped for several potential destinations which would bring us closer to Tibet: Wuzhou, Guilin, Kunming, Chongqing, and Xian, so that we could see the Terracotta Army. It was a bit of a guessing game, since we had no idea where we were going, or where any of these places were in relation to any others. For people who largely travelled without a plan, it was both annoying and frustrating. The longer the list of cities, the more expensive the travel permit became. In the end, it was expensive and time-consuming, but painless.

Our next task was to find the right place from which to purchase a ticket out of the city. We randomly decided on Wuzhou, which seemed to be in the correct direction - west. The dock was easy enough to find. But the ticket window was not. In a disappointing reenactment of the dal story of India, everyone we approached to ask directions to the window for Wuzhou failed to understand us. We drew a huge crowd, most of whom just stood and stared at us. And not in a good way.

Finally, a young boy propelled himself through the crowd and made his way toward us. He spoke only broken English, but suggested that we try window number ten. It was the right window, and in ten seconds flat, we had our tickets to Wuzhou. We had to compare the Chinese characters against the ones in our guidebook when we got back to the hotel, just to be sure, but they were all good.

It was roughly a 17-hour overnight trip, but it passed without incident. And food. So we went to sleep hungry. The food situation in China was disappointing. Anything vaguely western, such as toast, was a waste of time and taste buds. And you could never be certain exactly what was in the local cuisine. The term 'chicken' covered a very wide range of whitish, meaty textured ingredients. It looked like chicken. It acted like chicken. But it could have been anything from snake to dog or cat. The unfortunate lack of identifiable food was beginning to form a pattern that, at five months pregnant, didn't set a good tone for the rest of my Chinese adventure.

I woke with a start at around 9 a.m. the next morning to find James in a panic. 'Everyone is getting off. I have no idea where we are. It must be Wuzhou. Quick. Get up. We have to get off.' It wasn't a great start to the day. Hurriedly, we threw our belongings back into the backpacks, and disembarked. We still had no idea where we were.

With the help of our trusty guidebook, we managed to communicate our destination to some locals hanging around the pier. This time it worked a treat. We were led straight to the right window and handed two tickets with minimal fuss. Until they told us the price. It was astronomical. These were not local-priced tickets. We were definitely in the wrong place, buying tickets for the wrong form of transport.

A middle-aged Chinese man stepped out of the crowd to come to our rescue. It seemed we attracted crowds of mesmerised onlookers wherever we went. It was hard to believe the country could have remained so isolated this far into the twentieth century. It was like they had never seen foreign devils before. But we clearly interested the crap out of them.

Our new-found 'friend' spoke excellent, broken English, a surprise and a first. Plus, he was super helpful. He argued for a while with the ticket seller, who finally agreed to cancel the tickets he had just written out for us and refund our money, in *Renminbi*, of course, even though we had paid in FEC.

On our way to the next ticket booth, one for a local bus this time, our friend, Mr Wu, made polite and pleasant conversation. He even accompanied us to the hotel and waited outside for us so that we could go to lunch together. Though we were a little suspicious of his intentions, he was so helpful that we felt compelled to work with him. It was the lesser of two evil options.

Over a dismal lunch experience, we became aware of his ulterior motives for befriending us the way he had. He didn't like his job and, instead, wanted to be a tour guide. He had a plan. It involved us hanging around on the docks looking lost and pathetic. He wanted our situation to be so publicly recognisable that he would also be 'noticed' when he stepped up to intervene. It didn't work. A lot of people stopped and stared at us, but no one thought to approach us. They kept their distance. Even after we had paraded ourselves up and down the riverbank looking suitably pitiable for over an hour. We thanked him for all he had done for us, and left. Alone.

Back at the hotel, we found our concierge to be equally attentive. Every so often, he would pop his head into the dorm room and practise his pidgin English on us. He offset the intrusions by appearing with a pot of steaming Chinese tea and refilled our cups till we were so waterlogged we spent most of the night getting up to go to the bathroom. Add to that the fact that the whole hotel was freezing and I was suffering from pregnant bladder, and you get the picture. My own version of Chinese water torture.

Our bus left at 7 a.m. the next morning. Chinese regional transport had a habit of waiting for the vehicle to fill up before it went anywhere. This could take anything up to an hour or more before someone in charge made the decision to cut loose. Usually, by the time the bus or jeep or car left, it was hideously overcrowded and a thousand times more uncomfortable than necessary.

We left the Wuzhou bus station only a few minutes late on this occasion, since the bus had filled quickly. Although we weren't the first to board, we were surprised to find the very front seats empty. We hurriedly claimed them. We had already spent too many trips on Asian buses bouncing off the roof above the very back row. It wasn't long before we realised why these seats were undesirable. It was a cold, wet day, and they availed us of gale force winds and sleet at every pit stop and pick up point along the route. And these were often and many, respectively.

It only took eight hours in driving rain to reach Guilin. We couldn't see the brilliant limestone peaks that Guilin was so famous for rising above the Li River as we neared the city. They were shrouded in fog and rain. A bit like ourselves at that point.

TWENTY-SEVEN

Tweedle Dee
and Tweedle Dum

THE WEATHER REMAINED THE SAME as it was on the day of our arrival for the whole time we were in Guilin. Freezing. Wet. Foggy. Miserable. It was probably because it was late January, the thick of the northern hemisphere winter. We had to do something about our lack of warm-enough attire.

We found a little shop, a bit like an army surplus store. It sold all manner of coats. Colour choices were navy blue or khaki green. As if the greyness of the landscape wasn't depressing enough. We chose two oversized, double-breasted, knee-length khaki coats, padded with what appeared to be cotton wadding. And lots of it. They were just the ticket. But they had the unfortunate effect of making us look about ten sizes larger than we were. Hence, for the rest of our tour of China, we looked like Tweedle Dee and Tweedle Dum.

If the Guilin weather duped us out of the beauty of it surroundings, it made up for it with its food and coffee. The South Cafe and Hotel, run by two British expats, served up excellent meals. The best we had found so far. The menu even had some vegetarian options.

Being pregnant, I was acutely aware of the need for decent nutrition. But all too often, I found myself eating whatever looked passable just for the protein. As a would-be vegetarian, that was tricky. I had resorted to eating chicken. But I'm sure that was a very loose description. It might have looked like chicken, but it had a completely different consistency. I was left to wonder exactly what it might have been, since the locals appeared to eat anything that moved. But I couldn't be wondering for too long. I tried to eat without thinking. I especially tried not to think about the little dogs and kittens I saw sitting forlornly in cages outside several of the local restaurants. We didn't eat at those ones.

We spent the rest of the day wandering up and down the foreshores of the Li River, and climbing up Fubo Hill. The only way to the top was via a steep staircase, and the baby booted me from the inside the whole climb. It was the first time he had made his presence felt. Up until now, it had been easy to ignore the fact that I was pregnant, apart from the odd bout of morning sickness. I had usually attributed that to dodgy food, rather than my body reminding me of my condition. I was often preoccupied with the busy-ness of travelling, which left little time to consider what was going on in my body. There was always something to organise; some journey to negotiate, visas to arrange, or an accommodation fiasco to sort out. I suppose that was a good thing, because large chunks of the pregnancy had just happened despite me. Until now. That first kick from within brought it all home in a rush. There he was, working at growing while I worked at living. I started to notice that I couldn't sleep on my stomach any more. The baby bump was definitely there. The baby was there. For some reason, that surprised me. I got out the *Everywoman* book again. But this time, I marvelled over the week-by-week pictures.

When we finally reached the top of the endless stairs of Fubo Hill, I was less than well-disposed toward the murky view. After all the trekking we had done in Nepal and India, it should have been a breeze. But, it wasn't. And the monstrously heavy coat didn't help.

The whole city was surrounded by magnificent limestone pinnacles that burst upwards from everywhere in every direction. It would have been a truly awesome vista when the sun was out and the sky was blue. But we were not afforded that delight. The day we clambered up there, everything was grey - the ground, the river, the buildings, the clouds. We couldn't even see the sky. It rained often. All in all, it was depressing.

Trying to get out of the city was also depressing. We were in the middle of the Spring Festival, also known as Chinese New Year. Everyone in China was going somewhere to be with family. Trains to everywhere were booked solid. We abandoned the idea of heading to Kunming for this reason, and settled instead on Beijing.

I would be lying if I said we came to that decision on our own. Most of our travel plans were derived from others that we met along the way. We had no real plan. If we met someone who recommended a particular place, had just come from somewhere amazing, or who was heading off to an awesome destination, we would often go along for the ride. We didn't necessarily travel together, but we researched the possibilities and adapted accordingly. The idea of making for the capital came to us via two young Brits, Trevor and Kate, who had already spent quite a long time on the road. This time we teamed up to defeat the Chinese ticketing juggernaut that controlled transport prices.

The journey to Beijing was a mind-numbing 33 hours if the train managed to stay on schedule, a doubtful proposition in the heavy snow storms that were taking place in the centre of China. There was no way I was going to get on a train where I had to sit in a seat for that long.

There were two main problems associated with purchasing the tickets. The first was the price. As foreigners, we weren't allowed to buy at the local price. And we weren't allowed to buy them with local currency. So the enterprising Guilin people had come up with a workaround to help us out. Someone would go to the station and buy the sleeping berth tickets for us, at the local price, on one condition of sale - we had to pay for them with the precious FEC. We discovered the reason for the demand for FEC after agreeing to such a transaction. The so-called Friendship Stores would not accept anything else. And the local Friendship Store was the only place to buy coveted imported goods or products made only for export and not available to the general Chinese public. Ah so!

The second issue with the tickets was the way we had obtained them. So here we were, not allowed to buy local-priced tickets, yet boarding a train with exactly that. It begged the question, 'How did you get these?'

We had heard nightmare stories of people being refused boarding, or worse, being thrown off the train at the next middle-of-nowhere station. So, our cunning plan was to arrive at the station at the last minute to minimise the chance of a ticket check prior to boarding. It didn't work. Our tickets were checked at the door of the carriage. But they didn't even raise an eyebrow on the uniformed guard. He waved us on board with his gloved hand without comment. Phew.

The train departed at 1:15 a.m. so it didn't matter that there was a strict lights-out policy enforced shortly after our departure, by a stern guard waving a flashlight in our faces. Having stayed up so late just to catch the train, sleep was a welcome option, anyway.

TWENTY-EIGHT

Big Chill on The Great Wall

SURPRISINGLY, VERY SURPRISINGLY, our train arrived in Beijing just five minutes behind schedule. We had travelled clear across the centre of China, past grey, industrial cities and villages, everything blanketed in a heavy coat of snow. It was quite the timetabling miracle.

Outside the railway station, Beijing was just as grey as everywhere else, but with much wider streets. These were full of buses and rugged-up people on old-fashioned bicycles. Crossing from one side to the other looked as if it would take about ten minutes. If you made it, of course.

In stark contradiction to the congestion on the roads, people waiting for buses formed orderly queues. Until the bus arrived. Then it was every man, woman and child for themselves. Babies were passed over the heads of those nearest the door and already inside. Presumably this helped ensure their parents were also allowed to get on board. In our massive green army coats, we took up far more space than the locals. It took quite a bit of effort just getting up the steps and finding something to hang on to.

One major way that Beijing differed from the rest of our experience of China so far was in the accommodation it offered. The local CITS office clerk had found us a dormitory room at a hotel without batting an eyelid. On the way there, we did wonder if it was back in Guilin, it took so long to reach. But the upside was, Kate and I had the entire 16-bed room to ourselves, a private shower room, and lots of lovely, hot water. It made a nice change from the often cavernous and draughty rooms we had encountered so far. It was also a pleasant change to be able to remove the heavy overcoat. I'll never forget Kate's comment when I did so - 'Oh my God! You aren't fat!' She couldn't have known how much that meant to me, and I didn't tell her. But secretly, I was overjoyed that she noticed.

Venturing back into the city, it quickly became apparent how vast Beijing was. The wide-open space that was Tiananmen Square felt as if it could hold the entire population of the city. It was bounded on all four sides by equally immense monuments - the Mao Mausoleum, the Great Hall of the People, the National Museum, and across the road, the Forbidden City. It would have been impossible to make out the edges had it not been for these massive buildings on its perimeter. However, in true Chinese tradition, the only splash of colour in sight were the huge red flags waving from the top of the Great Hall. The rest was a boring mixture of brown and what I had come to call 'China grey'.

Without too much trouble, we managed to find the tiny ticket office that offered tours to the Ming Tombs and the Great Wall for just a few dollars. And with even less trouble, we bought four of them, not even realising it was going to be the first day of the Chinese New Year. Woe.

The bus that delivered us to the Ming Tombs the next morning had no heating. The temperature inside was a refreshing minus ten. At least, that's how it felt on our frozen extremities. It was hard to appreciate the massive stone mausoleums we were looking at from the entrance to the Sacred Way. It was so cold. The souvenir shop, on the other hand, was cosy and warm. We spent most of the visit in there, eating candy and waiting for the braver members of the tour group to reappear.

At the second stop, we descended into the underground vault to see the place where the treasures of the Ming Dynasty had once lain. Now, of course, they had been removed to safer resting places. My memory of the Ming Tombs has more to do with jigging up and down on the spot to try and warm up my feet than it has to do with historical artefacts.

The Great Wall was crowded with locals, out for the New Year holiday. They flocked to the restaurants at the base of the Wall, which extended for hundreds of miles in each direction, left and right. We had brought bread and soup with us so that we didn't have to compete for yet another horrible meal. We set off immediately up the stairs.

The climb was steep and relentless. Up and up, with the odd level platform and rampart, the lower ones populated by fierce-looking guards. We climbed as far as we could before the stairs crumbled away on the peak of one of the hills. The view was magnificent. All the post cards I had seen depicted a verdant green countryside, with the Wall snaking its way across the back of the ridges. It was nothing like that in winter. The Wall still snaked, of course, but the surrounding landscape was brown, treeless and disappointingly drab.

We found a place to seat ourselves on the stone steps without freezing our butts, almost, but the wind chill was a killer. When we opened our thermos, once full of hot, steaming soup, it was almost solid. Frozen solid. A bit like us. The bread had also gone hard in the plummeting temperatures. So, it was another poor meal. We stayed as long as we could bear the cold, which wasn't that long, then returned to wait in the bus for the driver to reappear.

If you're starting to get the impression that I wasn't particularly fond of China, you would be right. But my judgements were unfair. It was just the wrong time to be in such a cold, inhospitable place. China may well have been a more colourful place at other times of the year, but in the middle of winter, everything was grey. Even the mood of the people. Many of them wore big white surgical masks to protect them from the cold, and the air. Most of the locals rode around on bicycles. The air was horrid to breathe, thick and polluted. And also grey.

I also had the baby to think about, and it made me more irritable than usual, less forgiving of inconveniences. I thought about him a lot. I knew it was a boy. The red ribbon on the mosque had pretty much sealed the deal. But was he getting enough sustenance? I knew I wasn't. Was he growing as he should? Would he be strong? Would he be healthy? Would he have all his fingers and toes? All the things that go through the minds of parents-to-be. Granted, most pregnant women didn't have to deal with crowds so tight the buttons were ripped of their coats as they walked down the street; or buses so jam-packed they had to stand nose to back of neck with a man who smelled of garlic and diesel fumes; or stand behind a table of restaurant diners for two hours just to get served a decent meal.

No. It wasn't easy. China wasn't easy. They say what doesn't kill you makes you stronger. Well... I felt like I was running several marathons end to end. And more than just *my* life depended on me winning.

TWENTY-NINE

Breakfast in Beijing and How much is the Trans-Siberian?

AFTER SEVERAL DAYS' STAY in a cold and sterile hotel dormitory, the four of us were determined to find a decent Western-style breakfast somewhere in Beijing. We'd had several weeks of toast that shattered like a glass windscreen when it was cut, chicken that was just fat and bones, and pork, snake and dog masquerading as everything else. Properly-cooked eggs on real toast would help.

We arrived at the dining room of the Beijing Hotel at 8:31 a.m. At the time, it was the largest and most luxurious of all Beijing's accommodation facilities, so there was a chance of recognisable, western fare in the hotel restaurant. But even though it was officially open, according to the sign at the entrance, there was no one to be seen in the ballroom-sized hall. A diminutive woman dressed all in white from her face mask to her plastic wellies appeared, carrying a tray of cutlery and serviettes, and continued setting the closely-packed tables. She didn't even pretend not to see us. Our voices echoed as we called to her across the vast, high-ceilinged room.

'Excuse me. Can we get some breakfast?' She stopped what she was doing and looked up. There was no reply, not even a semblance of understanding.

'Breakfast. Breakfast? Breakfast!' We tried several different nuances of tone to see if anything twigged. Finally, she waved a white, gloved hand our way and said that magic word, the one that solves all problems when dealing with big noses, *'Mei-you!'*

But we were old hands at this now. Not to be put off, we sat down at one of the tables which had already been set for four. She pointed at her watch and repeated her catch cry. We pointed at the clock on the wall, which indicated breakfast was on for at least another twenty-seven minutes. She reiterated, louder. We refused to budge, having become fully aware of the significant power of flat refusal. She reluctantly walked over to our table.

'No have, okay? No have!' Perhaps she thought it would work better in English. 'We just want some eggs on toast. It's not that difficult and it IS still breakfast time,' we pleaded. She sighed heavily. 'Okay, two egg on toast.' She looked around the table, daring any one of us to order something different. 'For four,' she confirmed, and walked off. 'And coffee,' we yelled at her back.

When it did arrive, shortly after 9 a.m., two jelly-like eggs straddled an unbuttered slice of toast that looked like it would crack under their weight. And it was all cold. The coffee, on the other hand, was hot, and there was even a civilised jug of milk.

Trevor shook his head. 'Let's just take a train out of here. To Russia, or Hungary. Budapest sounds nice,' he said, as he filled our cups from the steaming pot.

I looked at him. 'You mean like the Trans-Siberian? How much would that cost do you think?'

'I have no idea,' he said. 'But we could at least be somewhere else for dinner.'

THIRTY

No Ducks!

WE DIDN'T GO TO BUDAPEST on the Trans-Siberian, or catch any other mode of transport out of Beijing. After spending the rest of the morning at the railway station, it proved to be more trouble than it was worth. And more expensive than we had imagined. But we did resolve to get a decent meal at least one more time during our visit to China.

That night, the four of us tried a restaurant off Tiananmen Square, highly recommended for its Peking duck dishes. When we arrived, it was not only full, but every table was surrounded by the next generation of dinner patrons, patiently waiting for those seated to finish. And everyone else was Chinese. We stood just inside the entrance, watching in amazement as waiters and waitresses moved swiftly and effortlessly among the tables. They balanced ducks, accompaniments and huge pots of Chinese tea on their arms. One suddenly passed quite near to us and hissed in our direction, 'No ducks!'

We looked at each other and laughed at the total denial of this statement. The old Game of Flat Refusal. Some seated diners called to us and pointed towards the ceiling. 'Foreigners upstairs.' We had heard of this quaint Chinese custom, but had never been victims of it before.

We had discovered that many restaurants were tiered from the bottom up. Entry-level dining was often unseated at large round Laminex™ tables. It was dining at its most basic. Patrons usually ate with their bare hands, throwing bones and scraps on the bare table. At the end of the meal, a waitress came along and wiped all the leftovers into a ceramic chamber pot that lived under the centre of the table. Then kicked it back underneath. Without emptying it. It was gross, disgusting and incredibly unhygienic. Watching her do it made me gag.

On the first floor, the process was similar, only the diners had chairs and no chamber pots. Food scraps were actually removed, and not just from view. The second floor and above was reserved for foreigners and favoured guests, who even enjoyed the luxury of tablecloths. Of course, the price also increased on each level.

This restaurant was quite famous and popular with the Hong Kong Chinese. The ground floor was jam-packed with tables and chairs. We decided to just play dumb.

We took our places in the crowd on the fringes of the room, and waited. When the next table of diners rose to leave, we charged. Unaware of the finer points of seating protocol, we found ourselves outrun by a band of fellow patrons who had swooped in from less distant realms, all jostling and yelling in Cantonese. Not to be discouraged, we each took a place behind one of their chairs. We would just have to wait till they were finished. It only took an hour and a half.

As we finally took our own seats, a passing waitress whispered to us, 'Okay, one duck!' She held up an index finger to emphasise her point, and to silence our vocal objections.

I'm not sure if it was because of the effort we had put in to get behind a seat, or the solidarity we had shown in refusing to budge for over two hours, but when our one Peking Duck with all accompaniments and free Chinese tea finally landed on the table, it tasted out of this world. The restaurant was truly worth its reputation. And the wait.

We had won this minor victory and it was sweet, even if we would lose every battle tomorrow.

THIRTY-ONE

Five Days on the Yangtze

CHONGQING, LOCATED IN THE GEOGRAPHIC HEART of the country, was not my favourite Chinese city either. We arrived from Xian at 9 a.m. one Thursday morning in February, drained and dishevelled from another thirty-hour train trip. The city was cold, confusing, hilly, and our map seemed pitifully inadequate. Nothing was where it was supposed to be, and no signs announced the way to anywhere. To make matters worse, it was as if the locals had never seen a tourist, and rather than answer our pleas for help to locate a hotel, we met with vacant but curious stares. Then it started to rain.

The rain deterred us from any sightseeing and the people deprived us of any privacy. It rained for the whole of our time in Chongqing, which was largely an inconvenient and frustrating transit stop. From here we would catch a boat all the way down the Yangtze to Shanghai, passing through the famous Three Gorges. If only we could find the ticket office and the boat in time. This had become a recurring theme in China.

Of course, it was still raining, and dark, when we caught a trolley bus to the docks on Friday morning. There were several vessels lined up along the banks of the river in various states of loading and unloading, but typically, no indication of where any of them were going. We paddled up and down in the soggy sand on the banks of the river, waving our tickets and chanting Wuhan. Apparently, we had to change boats in Wuhan, or Hankou, as it was also known. We seemed to be the only ones who knew it as Wuhan, judging from the blank faces.

When we finally located it, at the far end of the line, the boat was a dismal sight. The smell of diesel swamped us. A couple of long planks linked the gunwale precariously to the dock. Because of the way it swayed every now and then, it didn't look quite safe, although a stream of local men hopped nimbly back and forth delivering boxes of squawking chickens.

Cheap tickets on the boat meant fourth class, a twenty-four-berth cabin on one of the lower decks. It was dimly lit by bare fluorescent tubes which only deepened the dingy green of the walls. Lining each wall were six sets of double bunks set end to end and, except for one on either side just shy of the middle, they were already full. There was no option but to claim those two, and quickly. Our roommates were – surprise surprise – Chinese to a man. We, on the other hand, were not. And that was where the problems first started.

After numerous long and arduous train, boat and bus journeys from one end of China to the other, we had worked out that music preceded important announcements, which were always in Mandarin, and sometimes replaced them completely. This was the case with the mealtime melody. In lieu of any verbal information, breakfast, lunch and dinner sittings in the upper deck dining room were announced musically. A ridiculous little tune signalled the galley was open for business and a comical line of black-haired passengers began filing past our door, bobbing along in time to the rhythm.

Once we had worked out this musical call to action, we took our place in line for the restaurant. When we finally reached the buffet, however, the fare on offer was less than disappointing. For vegetarians, wary of anything vaguely resembling meat, there was only one choice - rice soup with the odd sprig of greenish cabbage lookalike vegetable. It tasted a bit like stewed old footy socks, not particularly appetising, even though we hadn't eaten for a couple of days. After the first tentative mouthful, it went over the side of the boat, back to the water from whence it most likely came. We had brought a few snacks on board with us, vaguely familiar cookies and lots of boiled lollies. They staved off hunger, but they didn't have much nutritional value.

Because I was roughly five months pregnant, it was inevitable that at some stage I was going to have to visit the little girls' room. I put it off for as long as I could but eventually I had to make the trip. When I entered the room, it was bustling with activity, more like a communal craft bee than a toilet. There were five little cubicles without doors, and they were separated from each other by a low retaining wall about as high as one row of tiles. Clearly, walls would have discouraged the active conversations that were taking place. I stared aghast at the conditions I was facing and the hundreds of eyes upon me, then turned tail and fled back to the dormitory without relief.

Finally, I could wait no longer. This time I knew what was ahead of me, but I was out of options. A crowd of expectant onlookers followed me in, then stood and stared as I squatted on the launch pads. There was much discussion in Chinese, probably about whether I was going to be able to manage a squat toilet, and when I did, much gaiety and nodding of heads. It was something I just had to get used to over the next five days, and it happened about every four hours.

I passed the time in our dormitory cabin by writing in my journal and knitting baby clothes. The woman in the bed opposite and above mine watched me like a hawk, talking animatedly with the other women in the room. I was knitting a jumpsuit, not a particularly complicated pattern, but not just straight knitting stitch either. After about an hour, she jumped down from the bunk, tapped me on the leg and gestured that I should give her the needles. It was obvious she wanted to try it. I was nervous about handing over my work, but I did. I resigned myself to the fact that I would probably spend the next couple of hours unpicking whatever mess she made. To my great surprise, she knitted about ten rows in perfect pattern, decreasing stitches in all the right places, and handed it back with a huge smile on her face, clearly well-pleased with herself. Just another lesson in letting go for me.

We passed through the famous Three Gorges on this section of the river trip. When we headed out to deck to check them out and take the obligatory tourist pictures, once again, it was disappointing. The gorges might have been more impressive in sunlight, but as was so often the case in our winter tour of China, the day was overcast with a light drizzle falling. The peaks on either side of the river were largely greyed out by looming, low hanging clouds of fog. There were only a handful of people on deck. This was, after all, a means of transport for most of our fellow travellers, a way of getting from A to B. And they had probably traversed the river many times over. For them, it was no tour, with nothing of interest to gawp at on the way - apart from us, of course, the resident big noses.

We spent three days in that dingy cabin with those 22 other people, none of whom spoke a word of English, but seemed more than happy to spend their entire day talking about us in Chinese. It was frustrating and disconcerting at the same time.

On our very last day on this boat, one of our fellow cabin members approached us. He was a tall thin man with spectacles and a kindly face. He hesitated at first, and then said, 'We hear you speaking English.'

Well, my mouth fell open in disbelief. It was all I could do to restrain myself from hugging him. 'Do you think you could help us to get some food?' this being the only thing racing through my mind at the time. His name was Mr Lu and he was shocked that we had not eaten, assuming that we had been filing past the wilted cabbage water and picking out dubious dishes along with everyone else. He hastily agreed to sort something out, and disappeared. Within about ten minutes, he returned with the Director of the Ship Unit, an egalitarian name for the guy in charge of the boat, who had in his hands the Holy Grail - a menu.

We were asked to order and to nominate a time we would like to eat. How about now? And at the appointed time, we were ushered into the dining room and served the two chicken dishes we had chosen and some toast. Oh, luxury. Why had we had to wait so long for this to happen? Why did he leave it till the very last day to speak to us? Who cared now. The food was delicious and the eight Yuan price tag irrelevant to the satisfaction it bought.

Mr Lu continued to be a gold mine of information and extremely helpful. When we docked in Wuhan later that evening he accompanied us to the correct ticket booth to buy our onward tickets to Shanghai. He and his travelling companions also helped us find a hotel for the night by escorting us on the bus, and refusing to leave until they had ensured we were settled into a dormitory room. Though it couldn't be called the Ritz by any standards, it was clean and warm. For the first time since we had entered China, I marvelled at the kindness perfect strangers had shown us. It was a welcome change from the apparent lack of care we had experienced till now and it occurred to me how incongruous and inconsistent this country could be.

The prospect of spending another three days on a boat now seemed just a little less daunting, knowing that Mr Lu would be somewhere on the same boat and ever ready to assist us. God love him.

It was much easier to locate our next transport vessel. The docks in Wuhan were rather more organised than those in Chongqing and the ship's crew seemed much more conversant with the ways of the foreign devils. They greeted us with welcoming smiles, and directed us to a cabin on the top deck, far away from peering eyes.

Mr Lu found us quite quickly, even before the boat had left the dock, and made sure that our eating arrangements were set up in advance. He told us that for the princely sum of six Yuan each, we could have our meals served to us in the cabin. Rather than jump in and order for the entire journey, we decided to take it one day at a time. This turned out to be the right decision since the first meal proved to be enough for several days. They just kept reheating it and bringing it back to us at each meal time. The worst part was the crowd of faces clustered at the entrance to the cabin, watching us eat and commenting on what was probably more food than they would see in a week.

Once we had sailed, it was pretty much the first journey on rinse and repeat. We sat on our bunks during the day, reading, writing and knitting while 22 pairs of eyes watched our every move. Turning in for the night was a welcome reprieve from the lack of privacy. But even that was doomed to be disturbed.

I had a lower bunk towards one end of the cabin and the man above me had shoved his duffel bag under my bed before climbing up into his own. Immediately, he started snoring at the top of his lungs. It was hard to get to sleep with the racket he was making, but after a couple of hours, it was the noise below me that drew my attention and concern.

At first it was just an indiscriminate shuffling noise, but it grew ever louder and began to sound like clawing and scraping. Using my torch to search for the origin of the sounds, I peered over the edge of my bunk. The zippered duffel bag was now half open, revealing its awful contents. Turtles! Full-grown, hungry, desperate-to-escape turtles. A couple had already succeeded in freeing themselves and had made it halfway across the cabin floor. Anything to escape being turned into turtle soup, I guess.

Hurriedly, I began banging on the bottom of the bunk above me until the snoring occupant woke up. He understood quickly what had happened. Some things don't require translation. Expertly, he scooped up the escapees and locked the poor creatures back into the bag. It was a long night, but in the morning, he derived great joy from telling his story over and over to all passengers within a four-cabin radius of ours, who laughed uproariously with each retelling. I just felt sorry for the turtles all the way to Shanghai.

It was a great relief to finally get off the boat, though it had taken forever to navigate the Yangtze delta. The main waterfront street, named The Bund, reminded me of pictures I'd seen from the early twentieth century. The brown concrete buildings were strong and rectangular, and reeked of Western architectural influences. It was almost like stepping into the past.

These days, Shanghai has become a world class shopping destination, full of brand name stores selling designer labels. But in 1984, no such thing existed. The biggest store in town was the Number One Department Store, and it was frightening archaic. There was little of interest to purchase, unless you were a factory line worker who needed a uniform and some tinned food that looked like it might have been stored on the ark. It was depressing.

It was around this time that we agreed it might be time to get the hell out of China. But the Shanghainese weren't going to make even that easy for us. And in the end, it required quite an elaborate workaround. China had taught us nothing if not how to think on our feet.

THIRTY-TWO

No Sleepers on This Train

IT DIDN'T SEEM TO MATTER WHERE WE WERE GOING IN CHINA, every trip was a long one, sometimes as long as 36 hours. On a train with a third-class seat, that meant 36 hours of pure hell. Similar to India, actually. We planned to leave Shanghai by train, and travel back to Guangzhou. Six weeks in the Chinese winter had just about exhausted our usual resourcefulness, and it was time to find somewhere else to go.

But the ticket Nazis at Shanghai Railway Station would not sell us a sleeping berth ticket. Even the little man who spoke some English and decided to try to help us could not. They just flatly refused to sell us tickets to anywhere in any class, directing us to the local CITS office. Buying local-priced tickets there, with local money instead of FEC, was, of course, impossible.

But there seemed to be no other way to get out of Shanghai by train. So, with the help of our new-found friend, we located the office and bought seat tickets to the small city of Hangzhou, just a couple of hours away, where we hoped we would have more success at the next ticket office.

As an overnight transit stop, Hangzhou was quite beautiful. In fact, it was the only day the sun shone in China for the whole of our trip. We spent an afternoon wandering around the picturesque lake area and found a bed in a luxurious hotel dormitory. We even managed to get local-priced seat tickets to Guangzhou without too much bother, which we were hoping to upgrade once on board the train. All good, so far.

However, at the train station we were treated like royalty. The platform guards spied us lurking in the crowds and shuffled us out of the 'local' waiting room and into a smaller, less crowded one, where we were deposited at the head of the queue. Our tickets were checked several times by several different men in uniform. No one said anything about the fact that we had cheap tickets.

Then the train arrived and it was every man for himself. We broke ranks and headed for the sleeping cars, but again, the might of Chinese bureaucracy came crashing down on us and all sleeper tickets were claimed to be... you guessed it - *meiyou!* As it turned out, our unnumbered tickets couldn't even get us a seat in any of the overcrowded carriages. Since the train had originated in Shanghai, it was pretty much full by the time it arrived in Hangzhou. Despondently, I found a piece of floor space between two of the carriages, draughty and right in the way of everyone passing by, which happened frequently.

They say necessity is the mother of invention, and the thought of spending the next 30 plus hours on the floor of this ramshackle carriage forced me to come up with a new plan.

In Hong Kong, prior to our departure for China, we had been told by fellow travellers that we should have our student cards amended to say, in Chinese characters, that we were students in Taiwan. The Chinese regime being as bloody-minded as they were, were still convinced that Taiwan was part of China, and refused to believe anything else. We didn't have student cards, since we weren't actually students, but we were able to purchase fake lookalikes at a little hole in the wall shop in the bowels of Chungking Mansions. Following that, we asked our guest house host to simply write the words about us being students in Taiwan on a little strip of paper, and inserted it rather awkwardly into the plastic card holder. It did obscure some of the details on the card, but hey, whatever worked.

I'd never had occasion to use the student card in China, always nervous that I would be found out to be a liar and thrown in some local hell-hole gaol. I was very aware of it in the pocket of my oversized Chinese army coat when I approached a group of train guards and ticket collectors seated at a table in the dining car.

At first, I just begged them to give us a sleeping berth but, even in Chinese, I could tell the answer was no. So, I did what any self-respecting backpacker does in a sticky situation - I played the only card I had left, and pulled the fake student ID with the Chinese characters about being a student in Taiwan out of my pocket, and gingerly handed it over.

Instantly, there were loud exclamations all around the table, lots of questions I couldn't answer, and then - a ticket book appeared from the bag of the most senior ticket official. He jabbed at the hand-written characters on the card and began writing out another ticket, one that indicated a sleeping car and berth number. We all shook hands very roughly. They all charged their glasses. And I nearly fell over with relief, and exhaustion. It had worked. I wasn't going to gaol, I was going to bed, to sleep for the next 30 hours in total, fully-prostrate privacy. There was a God, after all, and he was on this train.

THIRTY-THREE

Post Script on China

WHEN WE GOT BACK TO GUANGZHOU, having criss-crossed and circled China for six weeks, we were old hands at getting things done. And not very likely to fall for the Flat Refusal approach dished out by reception staff in so many hotels. We had even learnt to write a few simple Chinese characters, and when we were really struggling to communicate, it paid off a treat. At the end of the trip, we were back at the same hotel in which we had spent our first two nights. Only this time, we knew there was a dormitory because we had stayed in it many weeks ago, after a monumental struggle with hotel staff. This time, we weren't going to be so easily deflected.

Politely, we asked for a dormitory room. Just as politely, we were told it was full. Humbly, we said okay, retreated from the desk, and took the elevator to the third floor, that being where the said dorm was located. We took a couple of other random backpackers with us. They were on their first day in China and didn't understand the way things worked. They were more than happy to follow along as we showed them the ropes. It was the least we could do for the poor buggers, knowing what lay ahead for them.

Surprise, surprise - the dormitory was completely empty.

Defiantly, I threw my pack on the floor and sat down on the bed. A hotel staff member had followed me in, chanting 'Dormitory full, dormitory full!' It made her look crazy.

'Well it doesn't look like there's anyone sleeping in this bed, so I'll just have this one. And if the dormitory is full, then you won't be needing me to pay for it,' I announced.

Instantly, she caved. She knew she was beaten. Foreign Devil Logic had finally prevailed in the Chinese Game of Flat Refusal. It had taken six weeks, but I had finally learnt how to play. The other backpacker I had rescued from the front desk stood with her mouth open. I smiled smugly, just like my Dad used to do when he knew he was looking at a lay-down misere hand in a game of cards. It was one of those rare occasions in China where, when you won the argument, there was nothing sweeter.

PART 2

AND THEN
THERE WERE THREE...THEN FOUR

THIRTY-FOUR

Travelling with Children

JAMES AND I HAD DONE A LOT OF TRAVELLING before we had kids. You know, the cheap, budget, backpacker kind of travelling. You didn't have much choice if you wanted to stay away as long as humanly possible on limited funds. I don't think either of us thought it would be any different after the kids came along, apart from the obvious changes of having to travel with toys and nappies. So, when well-meaning friends pointed out that having kids would somehow make us settle down and become 'normal', we thought they were the ones who were odd.

Once we had children, we had the outlook that if we went somewhere, so did they. If they weren't welcome, then neither were we. It was a philosophy that saved us from boring social interactions on many occasions, and precluded us from some that might have been interesting on others. But we made up for it by doing everything together, as a family. We never entertained the thought that the naysayers were right, that we might, indeed, be crazy. Taking the kids was an easy decision, because it was no decision at all.

Travelling with a child, let alone a baby, was unheard of in our circle of friends and acquaintances. But it was another wedge that separated us from our families. And one that they weren't particularly comfortable with. Defiantly, we stood by our decision, just as we had stood by our decision to have a home birth. That had all worked out fine. There was no reason why this shouldn't either. We could be very stubborn.

It started with a three-day bus trip from one side of Australia to the other, from Sydney to Perth, when Mani was just six weeks old. The amiable bus drivers were kind enough to let me keep his bassinet on a spare seat directly behind ours. Every time I heard the faintest sound from back there, I was out of my seat, tending to him - breastfeeding, changing nappies, or just bringing him forward to sit and sleep in our arms. Although the bus was mostly full, we were halfway to Perth before some of the passengers knew he was there.

Things went downhill when we arrived in Perth and began the search for accommodation. It seemed no one wanted to rent us a flat because of the baby. And it didn't matter how much I pleaded or begged, the answer was still a firm no. A couple of agents just hung up on me when I phoned about their advertisement. It was a low time in my life. I felt defeated. I didn't know how to resolve the problem, and all my travel experience and the things I had learnt couldn't help me.

Finally, on the last phone call I made, I broke down and cried, huge sobbing breaths down the line. The English voice on the other end must have felt sorry for me. She relented, and offered us the chance to at least have a look at the flat. When we met her, everything changed. She gave us the key and we moved in - with just one backpack and a bassinet. I think she was amazed by our story and the blind courage we had shown. Whatever it was, by the time we left and moved back to Sydney three months later, she was my biggest fan.

We picked ourselves up and moved to Tokyo, Japan, when Mani was just nine months old. That got the naysayers nervous.

'But, you have no job to go to. Where are you going to live? How are you going to survive? You can't even speak Japanese!'

It was true; all those were valid points, but it only made us more determined to make a go of it - and prove them all wrong.

We lived in Japan for over eight years, travelling for several months every year to one Asian country or another. Thailand, Burma, Nepal, Borneo, Korea, Hong Kong, Taiwan. We even spent a couple of months in northern Europe. By the time we left Japan to spend a year on a Thai beach, we had a daughter as well. Noa.

Our first few months in Japan were spent in a communal house with about 20 other people from all over the world. At one of our summer barbeques, I was bailed up by a young American who had recently married a Japanese girl. She was expecting their first child.

'Can I ask you a question?' he said. 'My wife is expecting our first child in a few months' time, and our house is literally filling up with all these things we need for the baby's arrival.' He looked confused. 'Yet, here you are, you've just moved half way across the world with a nine-month-old and a backpack. How on earth do you do that?'

I smiled. 'Well, I'll let you in on a little secret. You don't need much. And you certainly don't need a house full of things.'

And therein lies the truth. Especially if you want to travel with kids. You might have to learn a few new tricks. And you might need to breastfeed for longer than normal, because who wants to have to sterilise bottles on an Indian train. Mind you, I have seen people attempt to cook whole meals on board Indian trains, not just heat baby formula. You might need to keep replacing toys that end up being thrown out bus or train windows to see what happens to them. Ditto for shoes.

You might also find you have to defend your decision, as we did in the Himalaya. Of course we trekked with the children. Hell, on my first trek I had been only four weeks pregnant. I wasn't about to stop now. And while the Nepalis loved us for it and greeted our family with open arms, our fellow trekkers were not so hospitable. A French woman abused me for having a baby on my back, yet she, by contrast, was carrying nothing other than a sturdy stick. Her porter and guide had everything else. At first, I used to get angry at being judged so critically by perfect strangers. But then, I realised they were just ignorant of how it could work, and how fulfilling it was. Safety was always at the top of our minds. It was their problem. Not mine to worry about.

So, the stories on the pages that follow all took place once we were three, and then four, and cover a span of many years. Yes, it was sometimes harder than it might have been alone. But it was also more rewarding. Again, great risk for great reward. Travelling with children opens doors in the world that adults on their own might not necessarily find.

If you're thinking about it, I say give it a go. Just prepare yourselves well. You're in for one hell of a ride.

P.S. Our kids are all grown up now. One of them loves to stay at home. And the other just CAN'T stay at home. Go figure.

THIRTY-FIVE

Europe on a $2000

Shoestring

OUR TRIP TO EUROPE BEGAN DEEP IN SOUTHERN INDIA. We'd taken a private car up to Kodaikanal, a hill station in the Indian state of Tamil Nadu, instead of waiting for the bus. It had seemed too good an offer to be true - a private car ride for the same price as the local bus? My first thought was that there must have been at least 50 other people jammed into the back of the car. But no. It was just going to be us and two residents of Kodai. Unbelievable.

We arrived late in the afternoon, but because 'the season' had apparently just begun, we couldn't find a reasonably priced hotel room anywhere. We ended up sharing a small single with attached bathroom with a Dutch couple from Sri Lanka. Nothing is ever straightforward in India.

After also sharing our dinner table, we grilled them about the costs, pros and cons of a European summer holiday. By the end of the meal, we had pretty much persuaded ourselves that we could afford it. Even though our budget was a measly two grand. We would just have to see how far that would stretch, but we had become kind of experts in that field.

We spent the next day wandering around the hill station figuring out how to budget Europe into our plans. We hit upon the idea to cut costs by camping out and buying bicycles to get around. Plus, if we flew out of India before Mani turned two, we would get away with a ten percent airfare for him. Excellent. More savings.

Just over two weeks later, we'd hightailed it through Tiruchirappali and Madras on local buses, survived a 40-hour train ride across the heart of the country to Delhi, bought the air tickets, made a flying visit by bus to Kathmandu and back to tidy up some loose ends we'd left unravelled, and were ready for our overnight flight to Amsterdam via Warsaw in early June. Phew. It may have appeared that things moved slowly in India, but if you wanted to, you could still make mountains move.

And so, we flew to Europe.

THIRTY-SIX

Two Tickets to Chernobyl

THE NEW INDIRA GANDHI INTERNATIONAL AIRPORT smacked of misplaced extravagance. Underneath the cosmetic veneer, Indian bureaucracy and chaos still appeared to reign. The customs officers had managed to delay some of the passengers for our flight to Warsaw for so long, through no fault of their own, that the plane was 40 minutes late taking off. At least our Polish Airlines flight had waited for the errant travellers.

For the rest of the world, the Chernobyl accident was big news. But for two grubby backpackers and a toddler grinding their way around India without access to media of any kind, it not only didn't rate, it didn't happen. If a nuclear reactor melts down on the other side of the world and you never find out about it, does it matter?

The first I heard of Chernobyl was shortly after we boarded an Air Lot flight from New Delhi to Amsterdam via Warsaw. We had decided to factor in a quick tour of Europe before our son turned two, thereby avoiding the need to pay full fare for him. If I nursed him for the entire eight-hour flight, we only had to pay ten percent of the full-price ticket. Looking back at that decision, for comfort and convenience, it was totally foolish false economy.

But anyway, there was a *Time* magazine lying on my allocated seat, left over from the previous flight. Since it was around six weeks old, it had probably been kicking around on board that jet for a lot longer than that. And the cover story headline? MELTDOWN.

I went pale. I felt weak, like someone had sucked all the air out of my lungs and replaced it with another gas. What the? What's this? What's happened? Oh, my God! A nuclear accident? In Europe?

Great. We were headed right into the open mouth of the dragon. Poland was one of the worst affected countries for fallout, being right in the path of the wind that blew that day and for the next few weeks. We had tickets to Amsterdam with a one day stopover in Warsaw, paid for by the airline due to the big break between connecting flights. I resolved then and there not to go near the water - so no drinking, no teeth cleaning, no bathing, and no laundry.

As I was about midway through the cover story, the hostess came past checking seat belts were securely fastened, and discovered the toddler sitting on my lap. 'Why this child no seat?' she boomed, more an accusation than a question. Instantly, she started rearranging the neighbouring passengers. 'You!' she said, pointing at the two people seated directly in front of us. 'Move there!' She was big enough and ugly enough that resistance was futile, and dangerous. So even though we hadn't paid for one, Mani got a seat.

We landed at Warsaw's Oczie Airport at the ridiculously early time of 5 a.m. and it was cold, cold, cold. It took quite some time to complete the necessary immigration formalities. Then, because Air Lot was hosting our night in Warsaw, we had to rely on Polish bureaucracy to sort us out. Three hours later, we and three other unlikely tourists were guided on to a very large coach and delivered, very quietly by comparison with Indian buses, to Novotel Warsaw. As if the contrast in transport wasn't enough of a shock, our driver was a big man, with a big nose and a blue uniform that made him look more like an army captain than a bus driver.

After waiting for an eternity yet again, the desk clerks managed to find us a room, a very nice room, luxurious by backpacker standards, hell, by any standards. Hot and cold running water, a soft, soft bed, room service, a hotel brochure/guide, writing paper and breakfast, lunch and dinner included at Lot's expense. But it came with the dubious honour of toxic food and water. Radiation no extra charge. Rather than risk the contaminated tap water, for another 24 hours we lived on the stash of Indian well water we had brought with us from Delhi. How sad.

After a short recess soaking in our luxurious surroundings, we headed out to find the real Warsaw. A short bus ride took us to the Central Station tourist office, where the staff had little to no interest in assisting us with any practical information. So, left to our own devices we simply wandered around the main drag, discovering many tempting pastry shops, and stores selling various foodstuffs and useless commodities. The window displays were all the same - stereotypical pyramids with large intrusive price cards.

It was strange to feel so out of place in a city where we melted into the crowd, white-faced and Caucasian just like everyone else. Culture shock is so weird. It was an unnerving experience to be a foreigner in a country where nobody knew it until you opened your mouth. That was totally new for me, having spent my entire travel career in Asia, where I was so obviously a foreign devil. It was the first time in a very long time that we hadn't stuck out like the proverbial wherever we went, even in our own local neighbourhood.

The Polish people seemed very circumspect. A few even spoke to us, or tried to, recoiling to polite pleasantries that went no deeper than, 'English?' I was never quite sure if that was a question about my ancestry or my language skills. Clearly, I didn't speak Polish, so we both just nodded and went our separate ways, smiling incongruously. One thing that was obvious after spending so long in Asia, and a strange thing to notice I guess, was that people kept bumping into me, something that hardly ever happened in Asia, despite the crowds.

After a full day of walking, wandering, and discovering random Polish monuments and landmarks, by dinner time we were famished and decided to take a risk on finding something non-toxic on the dining room menu.

The dining room was rocking, but we found seats with a fellow backpacker, a young Canadian guy also heading for Amsterdam the next day. A huge tank of a woman appeared at our table, closely resembling the hostesses from last night's flight. She smiled as she announced the dinner menu in a voice that commanded attention. 'Roast beef, roast lamb or roast pork.'

I smiled back as sweetly as I could and replied, 'We're vegetarian.'

'Me, too,' the Canadian chimed in. We nodded in unison, all quietly pleased with our confession.

She looked aghast. 'What? All three of you?' It felt like we had committed a crime.

'Okay. You will have sauerkraut.' And sure enough, she delivered three massive plates piled high with greenish, noodle-like cabbage. Oh, joy! Sure that it had probably been boiled to within an inch of its life in the same toxic water I refused to drink, I couldn't bring myself to eat any of it.

After a night of luxury in a room with actual running water that we couldn't drink, bathe or clean our teeth in, we were transferred back to the Oczie Airport for our flight to Amsterdam with the definite feeling that we had missed out on something, fresh air and clean water the most obvious.

THIRTY-SEVEN

Copenhagen or Bust

WE SPENT OUR FIRST TWO NIGHTS IN EUROPE ON A BOAT called the Wu Wei, run by the Rajneeshis, or Orange People, as they were affectionately known. The boat was moored in a canal close to Amsterdam Station. But even at 40 Guilders a night for the rather unique sleeping arrangement, quaint though it was, it was well out of our budget if we hoped to spend a decent length of time in Europe. Once our tent arrived, sent by a friend still in Japan, our budget prospects rose considerably. We had been fortunate to spend our first two nights under a hard roof as the weather had been absolutely appalling - rainy and cold after southern India's steamy climate.

Shortly after moving in to our soft-sided accommodation, we also bought bikes. We were the proud owners of two flashy clunkers, brand new, but a little on the cheaper side of junk. They were deemed to fit the bill, even though we weren't too sure exactly what the bill might be. The dotty little old salesman, who looked about 100 years old and probably hadn't been on a bike in 50 years, assured us they would get us to Copenhagen.

We spent the next couple of days fitting ourselves out for that very ride. There was quite a lot we needed. A sturdy baby seat for the back of my bike for starters, and a couple of panniers for James to struggle with. Everything we owned, from the tiny gas camp stove to our clothes and backpacks, had to fit in there. We tied the tent to the back of Mani's baby seat. At the end of the day, almost all of it fit. The rest went in the skip at the camping ground. We made some ruthless decisions to make Copenhagen.

In the meantime, the Amsterdam we discovered from our two-wheeled vantage point was beautiful. We found leafy little lane ways beside quiet canals and centuries-old facades, Gothic cathedral architecture, ladies of the day - and night - tram travel, and how to live dangerously by riding on the 'wrong' side of the road and forgetting to look left instead of right when crossing. I was almost squished under buses and trams several times during that first acclimatising week.

So, it was going to be Copenhagen or bust. And our first stop was to be Utrecht, a smaller historical city about 40 kilometres south of Amsterdam.

All cycling in The Netherlands is easy. Ha! Not! It looks easy because it is all relatively flat, but that only serves to lull you into a false sense of security. There are special bike lanes on the roads, even dedicated roads marked with centrelines and sporting signposts with distances. But don't be fooled. There is always wind; specifically, a head wind. No matter which direction we rode for the next three weeks, it always blew against us. It got to the point where I dreamed of riding up a hill, just so I could go down the other side without having to pedal for a while.

Not far beyond the city limits, the countryside changed dramatically to farmland. The area was dotted with thirteenth-century castles and manor houses complete with moats and drawbridges. It was lovely. Every church steeple rang out a different tune on the hour and signalling bells on the quarters and halves. It had an older world charm and grace with a new world fashion trend. I found the Dutch architecture very appealing.

We stopped once or twice to feed Mani and water the horses, ourselves. Pulling the load we had on was enough for six draught horses in a strong breeze.

We reached Utrecht mid-afternoon and found a campsite after consulting the helpful people at the Triple V, The Netherlands' version of Tourist Information.

Armed with the map provided by the tourist information office, we spent the next morning bicycling around the backstreets and canals of Utrecht. It had a totally different atmosphere to Amsterdam - pretty but not quite as 'smashing'. Maybe the effect of spending a week in the country had diminished our ardour for canals and some of the novelty had worn off.

With sore bums and aching hands, we set off in the direction of Amersfoort in the late afternoon. Not surprisingly, there was a stiff headwind. The 17-kilometre ride took us a good two hours because of it. The final part of the journey involved a refreshing downhill run into the city, but there had been little to see but freeway between the two towns. There wasn't much more to Amersfoort either, a fact we learnt as we burned out of town early the next morning. It was an early start on empty stomachs until we found a supermarket that was open, and picnicked on bread and cheese in a municipal park in Hoevelaken.

The scenery had changed again. Now we were in the country, dairy cows and sheep grazing leisurely on either side of the bike paths. We even pedalled through our first real wood, a lovely pine scent in the air and so green and shady. Near Elspeet, we found a dirt track passing through the middle of the forest and revelled in the earthy smells, cheerful bird life and perfect peace of the atmosphere.

At Epe, we got our first glimpse of modern Holland, not so much different from a newish Australian country town - 'nice' houses on 'nice' streets, all centred around a 'nice' shopping mall. Our neighbours in the camping ground were all regular European tourists on short road trips across the continent. We met the guy camping beside us because of Mani's attraction to bikes, and he took us into the woods to meet the wild pigs, protected by law but unable to survive in what's left of their 'wilderness' without nightly food drops. He provided us with another perspective on Dutch society, one that's hard to get a handle on when you feel like a spy.

Our ride took us through rural areas not too much different to those at home, apart from the fact that the landscape was dotted with windmills. Turning off the main road, we followed a cobbled pathway that passed through hamlets, rambling estates and quiet, leafy lanes. In Lemelerveld, our so far uneventful trip came to an abrupt halt when Mani got his heel caught in the spokes of my back wheel. There was quite a bit of blood and screaming involved, which brought an elderly local resident out of his house to investigate.

In broken English, he insisted we accompany him into the house, where he made a phone call. This Dutch town was organised in small communal groups, each home having instant access to a community health centre, supervised by a nurse. She came straight over, from just beyond the back fence, and examined Mani's foot. He was in shock, for about 5 minutes, just enough time for her to insist we see a doctor. Our protests were pointless and within another ten minutes a doctor had arrived. By then, Mani had taken a belly full of breast milk and had fully recovered. The doctor arrived to find him leaping from cushion to cushion across the sofas. For the equivalent of fifty dollars, she bandaged his foot and we were allowed to resume our journey. It was a wakeup call for us and a reminder to put sturdy shoes on his feet prior to every ride.

It seemed that all the towns we passed through from there to the German border were pretty much the same and not that interesting at that, but we loved the thick green woods and the smell of pine as we rode. The crops around us had changed to wheat and potatoes which gave the land a different feel. At one point, we passed a military base and for a few hours, NATO planes were our frequent overhead companions.

Arriving in Winschoten was cold, wet and dismal. It was a larger town than any we'd encountered so far, lots of shops and suburbia. We discovered that we could train our bikes to Denmark ahead of us for just 18 Guilders. It sounded like a plan; send the bikes and hitchhike to reduce the cost. But when we approached the station office the next day, for some reason it wasn't possible. So we resigned ourselves to continuing the long, long ride, something we hadn't considered when we set out. Hell, it had taken us almost two weeks and we still weren't out of The Netherlands.

Leaving Winschoten again the next morning was still cold, wet and dismal, and following a bike path that took us across a quaint little bridge meant we somehow managed to cross the border between The Netherlands and Germany without passing an official checkpoint. Because I've always been a stickler for the rules, when I realised our error, I insisted we return the same way and take the correct road across the border so that our passports were officially stamped. So, we did. But the border officials didn't seem to care about two hapless Aussies with a toddler, riding their way around Europe. They only glanced at our documents and waved us on. Damn.

Though we made it to Germany and managed to find a camping ground on the edge of a town called Leer, we'd become less than satisfied with the prospect of such a long journey ahead of us. The folk at the camping ground spoke no English whatsoever, so I had to crank out my high school German and try to hold a conversation. I must say that for the most part, they understood what I was trying to say, even if I hadn't said it quite right. We only stayed one night and decided to head back into The Netherlands and put our bikes on a train heading in completely the opposite direction - to The Hague. We would continue the ride from there, down the Nord See Strand and into Belgium.

It took only three hours to train it from Groening to The Hague. It was nostalgic and a little sad to see more than a week of hard work on the bikes whizz past the window in a mere three hours. A feeling something akin to flying out of Lukla in the Himalaya, without the splendour. The Netherlands had been a pleasant experience, but we had seen enough of the countryside and just wanted to go somewhere different.

In true no-plan travel mode, we headed for Belgium, mainly because of the expense of getting to the UK via the Dutch shipping link. We estimated an extra four days from The Hague to Zeebrugge, so the cost probably worked out evenly overall. But the experience was worth it. We got to see Belgium, as well.

The rain that had put us to sleep in a soggy sleeping bag in The Hague was persisting when we woke the next morning, so we packed up the wet tent and sat it out in the washing room of the clubhouse while we dried our sleeping bags. When it eased slightly, we set off to Central Station to collect the coat we had accidentally left on the train. By the time we reached Delft, it was just starting to fine up. We had lunch there, a pretty town, quite old and 'Dutch' looking, whatever that is. We even bought a birthday cake for our picnic in the park to celebrate Mani's second birthday. He didn't care where we were, but he loved the cake.

We had intended to ride only as far as Brielle, but when we worked out it was only another nine kilometres to Hellervoetsluis, we rode on. The islands south of Rotterdam were dotted with nature reserves, 'beaches' and camping grounds, so a place to stay was not going to be an issue. The place we found was quiet and private with the best facilities we'd seen yet, and at a rate cheaper than most.

The next day we extended ourselves in the interests of making Belgium by nightfall. We fell short by only 15 kilometres and had to stay in a cheap and nasty, large suburban caravan park. We had spent most of the day passing by the Nord See Strand, a long boring asphalt-covered stretch of dark, rocky, waveless coastline. We also crossed the last of the islands to reach mainland Europe again. The islands were connected by ferries and bridges that doubled as dykes which controlled the water flow to the south-west. They were long flat affairs with little inspiration from any side.

The ride into Bruges only took a couple of hours, but we had to spend more than four hours running bicycle repairs. Flat tyres, two punctures and several wheel changes later, we finally arrived late in the afternoon. Bruges was such an old and charming city that we decided to stay and soak up some of the vibes of the medieval architecture. Though I had enjoyed our European adventure so far, it was markedly different from our Asian one. We were so much more isolated from the locals. We'd had only a couple of interactions with camping ground staff and other campers. It seemed so impersonal after the crowded, shared experience we had been used to. We didn't even meet any other travellers or backpackers. Certainly no one else riding bikes around the continent. It was strange to me.

The next morning, following a round of washing, we walked around the city trying to capture some of its flavour on film. It's leafy canals, historic buildings and busy market squares were so photogenic, it wasn't hard to do. By nightfall, we had packed up and left the city, and arrived in the coastal resort of Zeebrugge, ready for an early morning ferry departure for the UK, and Dover.

THIRTY-EIGHT

Just Off the Boat

BACK IN THE SEVENTIES, EVERY YOUNG AUSSIE I knew dreamed of travelling abroad, specifically making the pilgrimage to London. We counted our savings, budgeted ourselves to the wall every week, just so we could sooner rather than later afford the elusive one-way ticket. We never considered buying a return ticket. We had it all planned out in our heads. Work for the money, travel around Europe, work some more, travel more. Rinse and repeat until you get sick of it, and then come home.

I spent a lot of years living in the shadow of the green-eyed monster, watching a string of friends going off one by one, and wishing it were me. I always knew I would get my turn. But never in my wildest dreams did I imagine I would arrive in the UK on a bicycle, with a two-year-old on my back.

But that's exactly what happened.

Spoilt by the cycle paths of The Netherlands, Germany and Belgium, even riding off the boat that had ferried us from Zeebrugge to Dover was a near-death experience. Talk about the shape of things to come.

A giant roundabout stood between me and the entry to Dover township and the road which would lead us to London. So, as I'd done in Europe, I brazenly stuck out my arm to indicate I was coming aboard. On the continent, traffic entering a roundabout had the right of way, but in the UK, it was held by the traffic already on the roundabout. I quickly learnt that British drivers had absolutely no respect for that malarkey. The abuse was almost instantaneous. "You can't effin' do that!" greeted me from the open passenger window of the car that almost took off my front wheel. Okay. Lesson learnt. Quickly.

Lesson number two – should have packed even lighter. The road from Dover to London via the A2 switch backed up the side of those famous white cliffs. There was no possibility of pedalling. I pushed the bike and my 2-year-old passenger up the feeder road for hours in the hot sun. Mad dogs and Englishmen be buggered. Add crazy Aussie backpackers to the saying.

There wasn't much relief when we did reach the top of the cliffs. The A2 was mostly a broad, dual carriage roadway with very little shoulder. And trucks. Lots of trucks. Typically, one brushed by my right elbow about every five minutes, creating a slipstream that almost shook my grip from the handlebars every time. By the time we reached Canterbury, just on dusk, I had the forearms of a Norse God.

The next day we fared much better. We knew what we were in for and made it all the way to Dartford, over 80 kilometres to the west. I still can't quite believe it we got that far in a day. Just goes to show what a few good downhill runs can do for you. But, alas, on reaching Dartford, there were no camping grounds to be found. I refused to ride another 30 kilometres just to pitch our measly tent for the night.

No, I had a much better idea. When in doubt, ask Old Bill. If you can find the police station. The amiable young constable at the desk that evening scratched his head. "Hmm, well there may be some bylaw against it, but I can't think of one right now, so I guess you can put up your tent somewhere up on the heath."

Well. Excellent.

Problem. 'The Heath' was a setting straight off the pages of *Sleepy Hollow*. It was a large area of mostly flat scrub, dotted with dense low woodlands and criss-crossed by walking trails and bike tracks. We pitched our tent in the dark, crawled inside and waited for the nearest axe-wielding psychopath to discover us. Not one wink that night I slept, especially since I lay with one hand sticking out the door of the tent, firmly grasping the wheel of my bike. Just in case the axe-wielding psychopath decided to take it for a spin prior to murdering us all.

Sometime during the dark night on The Heath, I decided I'd had enough of this wild and potentially dangerous road trip. Spurred on by a new resolve, I insisted we find a nice little cafe, have a normal English breakfast...and break the cardinal rule of backpacking — ask a local. There is a very good reason why asking a local for help is against the unwritten backpacker code. It is never helpful. Often just the opposite. But desperation can play funny tricks on you.

So, against my better judgement, I trundled myself into a small travel agency with Mani on my hip. The fact that I hadn't showered or slept properly in several days most likely accounted for the way the jaws of the three elderly women at the line of desks fell open. Politely, I explained that I was trying to get to London and wanted to know another way, other than going down to the A2, which I was convinced led only to certain loss of limb and possibly life.

They looked at each other as if suddenly struck dumb by my appearance. Finally, one of them managed to find her voice. "By car?" she enquired. I went on to explain that I was on a bike. "A motorbike?" another asked, incredulous. "No. Actually, a push bike." That simple statement had the effect of a sonic boom, and in unison, they all slumped back in their chairs. When they regained composure, one of them said, "We always take the train."

Eventually, I convinced them to just write me a list of all the little villages and towns that we would pass through if we took the back roads. After much conference and discussion, they managed to make the list, all the while protesting that it was going to take hours and hours. And it did take hours. Two hours to be exact.

Eventually we met up with a main road again as we neared the outskirts of London, and discovered that the road to Victoria Station was littered with suburbs named after pubs you might visit on a night out in Sydney's Rocks area.

I always knew I'd visit London one day. But never in my wildest dreams did I imagine I would arrive on a bicycle. Apparently, neither did the British.

THIRTY-NINE

Ponta-WTF?

WE SPENT A COUPLE OF WEEKS BIKING AROUND LONDON, using a random camp ground in Hackney as a base. As British summers go, the weather wasn't too bad. It didn't rain that much, so camping turned out to be an okay option. The fact that it didn't get dark till almost ten at night helped enormously, a fact my friends had neglected to mention when regaling me with their UK travel stories. No need for torches while cooking dinner on our little one ring gas burner here, then.

But a trip to the local convenience store cum supermarket in Hackney high street, which seemed to always be frequented by young guys in hoodies, was a tad more dangerous. We had absolutely no idea that Hackney was on the top ten list of most dangerous areas in London, but after a few days in town, it wasn't hard to see why it had claimed that fame. Ignorance can really be bliss, eh?

Our time in London could be described more easily by ticking off the list of famous landmarks we hadn't visited, rather than those we had. I think we saw Big Ben from a distance, Piccadilly Circus and Trafalgar Square from the ground, and Westminster Abbey from the outside. It was only a couple of weeks before Fergie and Prince Andrew's wedding, so the place was locked up tight. Everything else had an entry fee and having blown in from India, pounds and rupees just couldn't be reconciled. We did go inside St Paul's Cathedral, but to be honest, I couldn't stop thinking about the Bible story where Jesus threw the moneylenders out of the temple, and wondering what he would think of this church. The place was a full-on market stall. Maybe we were just there on the wrong day.

As if to confirm my observation that we simply melted into the local population, one day we were stopped by a couple with a huge video camera. We were riding one of the few bike paths that led from Hackney to Central London. We had tried to find as many designated paths as possible just to avoid the hair-raising experience of riding in London traffic. These two were making a documentary, and asked if we would mind being filmed riding towards the camera. They were campaigning for more bike paths. Who wouldn't want that? We heartily agreed. But the thing that struck me was that they never asked where we were from. It was true that our accents had worn off after several years of travel and teaching English in Japan. They must have jumped to the conclusion that we were British. Either that or they just weren't interested, something we had learnt to deal with on our brief return to Australia. Often conversations never got past 'So where did you go?' Beyond that, not much. We never knew the outcome of the documentary, but the contact with them did help us to locate the London Cycling Campaign, who helped us immensely by selling our bicycles for us when we left London.

We had decided not to try and leave London by bicycle. The two weeks we had been there had shown beyond doubt that British motorists held little but contempt for two-wheeled traffic. But not to be labelled mainstream, we caught the Tube out of town a way, and stuck out our thumbs for a ride.

We had to wait for quite a while that first day, and it was hard to discourage Mani from throwing his lone toy out into the path of oncoming potential lifts. At two years old, it was the best game yet - Ma plays chicken without getting plucked! It didn't do much toward catching us a ride, but it did get us a lot of attention, not to mention, abuse.

We finally got picked up by a publisher on his way home to Gloucester, which was where we thought we were going. When our chauffeur discovered that we hadn't been in contact with the hosts we were expecting to spend the next few days with, in Gloucester, he insisted on driving us home to his place so that we could use his phone. That was lucky, because it turned out our friends had moved to Bristol, not far from Gloucester by Australian standards, but a frightful distance for a Brit who hadn't been anywhere other than Gloucester and London. After tea and biccies with the publisher's family, we caught the train down to Bristol, about 40 minutes away.

After that, everything pretty much went according to plan. Well, perhaps I should say, it went without hiccough, because we didn't have a plan. We didn't travel that way. We saw or heard of something that sounded marginally interesting, and we went with it. It didn't always work out, but we never suffered from itinerary burnout.

It did go smoothly, though, until we arrived in Swansea, on the south coast of Wales. I had pleaded with the young men who drove us there from Bristol to leave us on the motorway, since we had no real interest in going in to Swansea, and a much better chance of getting another lift outside town. We had hoped to get all the way over to Fishguard on the west coast, and catch a ferry to Ireland. Dreaming. But either they weren't listening or didn't care, and drove us into Swansea town centre. In hindsight, it was quite possible they thought it wouldn't be a good idea to leave us stranded on the side of the motorway on dusk, with a toddler. But we hadn't even considered that in our blind hope.

There we were in the middle of a city, with nowhere to stay, and no campground in cooee. Since it had worked relatively well for us before, I dragged out the old police station chestnut. We couldn't find one, but we did find a public phone box with a phone directory. So I called and put my question to the young lass with the lovely lilting voice who greeted me gaily on the other end of the line. Not a word single understand could I. She may have well been speaking Welsh - since we were in Wales, she probably was. I gave up and handed the phone to James. He had no success either. He hung up.

I love a challenge, always have. Plus, I was desperate. So, I called back. But it was all Greek, or Italian, or Welsh. I don't know. But I could not make out any of it. Despondent, we got on a bus, any bus, that looked like it might be heading out of town, in the hope that we might find somewhere awesome to pitch our little dome tent.

And that's how we ended up in Ponta-WTF?

FORTY

Crossed Wires in Cross Hands

THE BUS DRIVER HAD TO TELL US that we were at the end of the line because it wasn't immediately obvious. It didn't seem to be anywhere in particular, just some random tiny village with a row of farm houses, a bridge over a small river, and a single shop. The most noticeable landmark was the motorway that loomed above the landscape, cutting a swathe across most of it. It seemed ridiculous that many hours earlier we had been only minutes away from where we now stood. But we were still no closer to finding somewhere to lay our heads for the night.

After walking several hundred meters with Mani strapped to my back in his baby seat cum carrier, I approached one of the few houses that appeared to have a paddock for a front yard, and knocked on the door. It was close to dark and the lady of the house looked scared shitless as she opened the door. I explained politely that I was looking for a place to pitch our little tent for the night, and asked if that place might be her extremely large front yard. She just stared at me. And shut the door. I took that as a no.

Disheartened, we headed back the way we had come, aimless and without a clue as to what to do now. The merciless rebuttal had left me unwilling to try again at another door. If it had been just the two of us, I wouldn't have cared where we lay down. The side of the road might have been a last resort. But we had Mani to think of. The protective maternal instinct was stronger than my own comfort. There had to be a solution. And we had to find it, and quickly. It was almost dark.

We passed under the motorway again and this time noticed a small area of scrub, almost impenetrable, but perhaps offering shelter from the thieves and muggers that may wander by in the night. Suddenly I remembered our night on Dartford Heath with more than a little dread.

Back in 1986, Pontarddulais (pronounced *Ponta-doo-ee*) was a tiny village on the very fringes of Swansea. Looking on Google Earth the other day, I discovered it has become a largish city, complete with malls and car parks. In fact, the tiny patch of scrub we chose to pitch our tent that night is now a paved and landscaped park area which would no doubt be impossible to camp in these days.

But back then there were no such restrictions. We hacked our way into the undergrowth by sheer strength of will.

It was not a great night's sleep, with the roar of traffic overhead and swarms of mosquitoes around our ears. When we dragged ourselves out and back onto the road the next morning, crumpled and weary from the experience, we still had no idea where we were, or better still, how we were going to get out of there.

I found a pen and a too-small piece of paper and fashioned a sign of sorts that announced Fishguard as our destination. Hopeful, to say the least. Hopeful, but not particularly helpful. There was a bit of passing traffic that Sunday morning, mostly people heading to the one shop for their morning newspaper. But they were friendly enough and waved as they passed us for the second time, on their way home again.

Some even shouted, 'Sorry.' I think they knew we weren't going to make it to Fishguard that day, possibly even that week.

Eventually, after several mind-numbing hours, our luck finally turned, and a large, gold 4WD screeched to a stop just down the road from us. We'd been there so long that it took us a few seconds to realise it had stopped for us. Jack, the driver, was reluctant to leave us on the side of the road. Maybe it was the toddler. Maybe just that we looked so hapless, hopeless and desperate. Nevertheless, he found it somewhere in his heart to stop, and told us to get in. We didn't know where he was going, even though he told us. We didn't even know where we were.

He also told us we were not going to get a lift anywhere around here and that he would take us back to somewhere called Cross Hands on the main road. It wasn't too far away, and on the way, he explained all about life, the Welsh universe, and how long it might take us to get to Fishguard. But when we arrived at his workplace, everything changed.

Jack's boss was a small-town Mr Big, who walked as if his shoes were a couple of sizes too small. After a round of courteous introductions, Mr Big invited us in for morning tea so that he could hear all about our life story. It was obvious he was used to giving orders and getting his own way, so resistance was futile. I was instructed to make tea 'for the boys' and found myself staring down a huge urn and jars full of tea bags and sugar in a cavernous lunch room, sparsely furnished with plastic chairs and tables.

While we chatted, the Mr Big smoked and looked at his watch often, as if he had somewhere else he urgently needed to be. He barked out orders to anyone who entered the lunch room. Then he offered to drive us to Fishguard personally, and he wasn't going to take no for an answer, even though it was not high on our list of things we wanted to do. As it turned out, he couldn't drive. Jack was his driver, so, of course, it was down to him to drive us to Fishguard, a fact he looked less than happy about.

Now, you may think a journey of only 55 miles, roughly 90 kilometres, would take less than an hour. But no. It took the rest of the day, a full seven hours.

FORTY-ONE

Welcome to Dingle

BECAUSE IT WAS A SUNDAY, the pubs in Wales were technically closed. But the first one we came to, less than ten minutes from town, seemed more than willing to open for Mr Big. We were surreptitiously bundled in through a side door like thieves in the night, and soon the place was filled with people who appeared to be his friends. They all settled in for a good session. Once upon a time, I would have welcomed a Sunday pub crawl, but these days I didn't drink, so the scene quickly grew old. It must have shown on my face, because out of the blue, Mr Big rose, ordered a bottle to be placed in a brown paper bag, and announced we were on our way.

The next part of the journey was almost exactly as I had imagined Wales might be - green country lanes, rambling old castles with immaculate gardens and neatly-pruned hedgerows. Mr Big seemed pleased with the blend of whisky and the mild Welsh summer. He swigged indiscreetly from his paper bag and told us stories of his homeland. It touched him so deeply that he started to sing. Jack looked over his shoulder at us with a wry smile to see how we were coping with this turn of events. This was obviously not the first time something like this had happened.

Our next stop was on the pretext of lunch, and though Mr Big and Jack invited several friends to scoff steak sandwiches with them, it was largely an excuse for more imbibing. As a teetotalling vegetarian, the frequent diversions were starting to wear away at my ability to stay calm and polite. Mr Big had now had enough to drink that he would no longer notice any changes in my demeanour. He drank on regardless, waxing lyrical about his lovely wife, his wonderful family, and his thriving business. He offered us jobs as PR managers for a travelling circus and a healthy package of fringe benefits. Oh, yes, we jumped at that one. Not. Even Jack shook his head, and ordered himself a whisky. I mentioned again that we were hoping to get to Fishguard by nightfall, something that looked ever more remote as the day progressed.

Not long after we left our lunch venue, we picked up another hitchhiker, a young girl who wondered whether she should jump ship at the first opportunity when we told her how our day was going. Mr Big encouraged Jack to drive faster, and to pass other vehicles on the inside, a feat nigh impossible on either side of the narrow country roads. We drove deeper and farther into the Welsh back country.

We came to a stop at a tiny place that, from the outside, looked nothing more than a farmhouse and a few outbuildings. It was, surprise surprise, a pub and we were met at the car by an elderly, silver-haired gentleman chanting, "Welcome to Dingle, Welcome to Dingle!" over and over. A lot of people appeared from nowhere yet again, and Mr Big shouted the whole pub drinks. The tables in the lounge bar were jammed together to make room for a minuscule dance floor. There was a piano in the far corner, a well out-of-tune honky tonk sound coming from it, and the man playing it wore an over-sized, Mexican sombrero.

After serving everyone with a regal flair, including Mars bars all round for the children, Welcome to Dingle dragged me up to dance, staring deeply at me the whole time, and calling me Blue Eyes. We did a slow waltz to a fast jazz number, dodging between tables and patrons. If this place were real, it wasn't in Wales. Welcome to Dingle had never heard of Fishguard. Neither had the Mexican honky-tonk player, who doubled as the local undertaker. Welcome to Dingle seemed particularly proud of him as he told me he would bury four people the next day. I was beginning to think I might be one of them.

I found Jack staring into the bottom of an empty glass and decided it was time to take back control. I told him to simply point me in the direction of Fishguard and we would make our own way from here. It seemed to be the safer option at any rate, even though it was getting quite late. But then, Mr Big suddenly scrambled to his feet and left the pub without warning. We rushed after him. He led us back to the car, reminding us that this was the twelfth one he had owned. I wasn't sure if it was a threat or a warning, but it was obvious what had happened to the other eleven. We all clambered back into Car Number Twelve.

We drove straight to Fishguard Hospital, still a good 15 minutes from the dock, and waited yet again while Mr Big paid a visit to his cousin's nephew twice removed. Apparently, he had suffered a heart attack, most likely after hitchhiking in Wales.

The last boat to Ireland left Fishguard harbour at 6:15 p.m. At 6:05 p.m., we sped down the wharf like we were in a Bond movie, screeching to a halt right beside the gangway. Mr Big shovelled handfuls of one pound coins our way, most of which fell to the ground. Jack shuffled nervously. Awkwardly, and for want of something better to do, we shook hands.

All the way to Ireland, I scoured the map for a little place called Dingle in the wilds of Wales. I couldn't find it. It certainly wasn't on the map I had, and quite possibly, not on any map that ever was. To this day, I still don't believe it exists.

FORTY-TWO

Copenhagen at Last

WE TRAVELLED BACK TO AMSTERDAM FROM LONDON on one of those slick overnight Greyhound-type buses with a less than agreeable driver. It was full of British party animals who were falling down drunk and annoyed the driver the whole way, to the point where he almost threw them off the bus in Antwerp in the middle of the night. They were off to party in Amsterdam, but obviously had been unable to wait that long.

We arrived in Amsterdam early in the morning and decided that, since we had already spent some time there earlier in the summer, we would head out of town as quickly as we could. Only this time we would hitchhike out in the direction of Germany. The bikes were long gone, sold to the London Cycling Campaign for a sum close to what we had paid for them. So, there weren't a lot of options.

We found an official *liftplaats* on the outskirts of the city, designated by a large blue sign with a white thumb emblazoned on it. There were already a handful of fellow hitchers waiting for lifts when we arrived, early the next morning. One by one, they were all picked up by passing motorists and disappeared into the haze of the highway. But after spending most of the day waiting, by late afternoon we were still there. Hadn't moved an inch. Not even the presence of a toddler helped us attract a willing driver. It was starting to look like we might have to spend at least one more night in the city. The prospect did not thrill me. I was too depressed by the way the day had panned out.

We got talking with one of our fellow travellers, who was heading in the same direction. When a car finally stopped at his feet, he very kindly negotiated with the driver to take us along for the ride as well. It was so kind of him, and we were more than grateful. The four of us all squashed into the back seat.

The driver and his single passenger dropped us just over the border into Germany, and, as luck would have it, right opposite a vendor of the remarkable and tasty fries and mayo served up all over northern Europe. We ate them by the side of the road while we waited for our next lift. It was dark by now, and we were beginning to wonder if we might be pitching our tent by the motorway again tonight. There wasn't going to be any wild undergrowth to conceal our presence here, though.

Finally, a car stopped, occupied by two young Germans, who agreed to take us to Munster. It wasn't very far into Germany, but that was as far as they were going. As had been extended to us, we asked if we could also take our companion along with us. But due to the lack of room in the back seat, they declined. It was with a lot of guilt and just a hint of gratitude that we climbed inside at the insistence of the third wheel guy. We sped away, leaving him standing there. I felt awful.

The two young Germans could not quite believe that we were hitching with a toddler, and when they learnt that we planned to pitch a tent somewhere in Munster, they freaked out. A lot. Not being intrepid travellers of the same ilk probably accounted for their insistence on swinging by the local youth hostel. We freaked out a little bit at the prospect of having to pay the cost of a family room for the night, but fortunately for us, the Y was already full.

Reluctantly, they realised that we were determined to spend a night in the wilds of Munster, and drove us to a large park on the edge of a lake right opposite the said youth hostel. It was obvious this was not their first choice for us, but they stayed with us long enough to find a suitable site, pitch the tent, and make sure we were as comfortable as could be under the circumstances. They even left us their torch, because we didn't have one. Up to this point, the European daylight hours had meant we hadn't needed one.

When we bade them farewell and thanked them profusely, they insisted on coming back early the next morning to take us to the autobahn, from which we would be able to hitch north. The uncompromising generosity of strangers humbled me again.

From the spot on the autobahn where they dropped us, we waited and waited. There just wasn't much traffic and we didn't get picked up till around lunch time. A young girl, barely in her twenties, skidded to a stop in a shiny, dark blue Audi. Even though our sign announced that we were headed for Copenhagen, she offered to take us to Hamburg, or as close as she was passing on the freeway. It was a couple of hours north of where we were, so it was an acceptable target. Besides, we knew someone who lived there. Maybe we could catch up. But as usual, we hadn't planned for that.

Our driver was very quiet. I think once we got past the pleasantries of 'Where are you from?' and 'Where are you going?' she fell asleep. I kept trying to make polite conversation, if for no other reason than to keep her eyes open. The autobahn could be long, straight and boring, and a crash at over 150 km/hr was not high on my agenda.

As promised, she dropped us at one of the service station car parks just short of Hamburg late in the afternoon. We had a bit of a snack and didn't have to wait long for our next ride. Two young guys headed for the resort town of Scharbeutz on the Baltic coast saved us from a night on the side of the autobahn. It was only just over an hour's drive, so we arrived in the early evening, just in time to find a suitable, inconspicuous spot to pitch a tent.

It wasn't a great choice. But we hadn't had much time to decide. Pitching a tent in the dark is not fun. We had headed down a forest trail at the back of the main drag, found a small clearing, and got to work getting set up camp. It wasn't until morning that we discovered we were right beside one of the most popular running tracks around the upmarket resort. And every man and his dog came out early for their morning constitutional. Ho hum. At least we weren't underneath a freeway.

We couldn't afford resort-priced breakfasts, so we made do with some leftovers we had for Mani, and went out in search of the road to Copenhagen on empty stomachs. We were used to that by now. It was an inconvenience, not a disaster.

We lucked in with our next ride, which also turned out to be our last. The Israeli tourist couple who stopped for us were going all the way to Copenhagen, too, and kindly suggested we stay with them and their hire car, and resume our journey together once we docked in Denmark. As it happened, it was a trade-off.

For individual passengers, the fare was a minimal 18 Deutsch Mark per person. As passengers in a vehicle, the cost escalated to somewhere around 150 Deutsch Mark, regardless of the number of passengers. They asked us to share the cost, and we could hardly refuse. So, we had to pay half the cost of getting the car to Denmark. When we drove off the other side of the crossing, past all the other individual travellers trying to pick up lifts, we knew we had made the right decision. There were so many thumbing for rides from the offloading traffic, it looked like a long wait. It had been a small price to pay for a lift all the way to our destination.

FORTY-THREE

Home Sweet India

AFTER A COUPLE OF WEEKS SPENT WITH STEFAN, the Danish friend we had met in Burma, we returned to India, once again travelling with Air Lot via Warsaw. The Poles, in their wisdom, had not allowed us to leave the airport transit lounge this time, even though our connecting flight to India was a full 11 hours away. There was nothing to do but drink vodka, which most of our fellow passengers had done, so the flight back had been filled with the sound of retching, and a constant stream of drunks staggering up and down the narrow aisle. We weren't in the mood for the crowd of insane taxi and rickshaw *wallahs* waiting for us outside the airport doors in New Delhi.

It was very early morning, just on sunrise, the most beautiful time of day in India. The sun rises, bathing everything in a smooth golden shimmer, and the dust has not yet been stirred up by the teeming life on the ground. We opted for a horse and buggy ride into the centre of the city, and it was magical. So relaxing after what we had just left behind. It felt like we had come home.

Returning to India after two months in Europe was like seeing the country anew. All the little things so quickly forgotten came back to the fore. Everyday things like the faces of the old men in the pitiful, tiny street corner stalls, the chai shops, the cows wandering complacently in the streets, the blare of auto-rickshaw horns mixed with bicycle bells, the aromas from the myriad restaurants and mobile carts all strung with incandescents in the evenings, the blinding midday heat and the sticky, sweat-soaked feeling on your skin, the endless requests for *baksheesh* from beggars, the colourful bazaars, the exquisite saris with dusty hemlines, the grimy hotel bathrooms and slimy sluice buckets, the faces of the curious children. It was a total immersion experience that got right inside my head. It was familiar. And very welcome.

But the respite was short lived. The buggy deposited us at the massive iron gates of Mrs Calico's Lovely Guest House compound. It was a striking orange, cement-rendered building. A narrow archway led through into a central paved courtyard, where several elderly women stooped and swept with brooms made of bundles of twigs tied together. A couple of them noted our arrival, or more truthfully, the arrival of our son, with a sly smile, but kept on with their work.

Mrs Calico appeared in one of the many doorways, a large robust woman with ample hips and a voice that demanded obedience. She motioned for us to approach and led us into a darkened room, empty apart from four *char poi* beds and a low hanging light bulb on a cord. The windows had grills on them and the floor was bare cement - not very inviting, to say the least.

'This will do?' she asked, but left the room without waiting for an answer. James removed his backpack, and I set the baby carrier down on the floor and flopped down on the string cot. I hadn't lay there more than a minute when I suddenly rose and began scratching violently at the back of my legs.

One of the old woman sweepers passed by the door and saw me twisting and turning, clawing at my legs. Hurriedly, she pushed me aside, grabbed the cot and skull-dragged it out into the courtyard and began banging it up and down very roughly. A thousand tiny, black bugs fell all over the ground. She pointed at the ground and said something in Hindi which could only have meant 'Bed bugs!'

Mrs Calico suddenly appeared again and began ranting and raving about people bringing in the bugs from the Salvation Army Hostel in Mumbai. On and on she went, but I had trouble following her reasoning. After all, this was New Delhi, hundreds of miles from the Mumbai hostel. And why pick on the Salvos, when bed bugs could be picked up in any number of a million cheap hotels and guest houses around India?

Since our room was now empty, all the beds having been dragged into the courtyard for similar treatment, Mrs Calico hustled us into another room. It was already occupied by one bedraggled Canadian and a young Japanese man. The Canadian was reclining on his cot in the corner of the room, smoking a joint of hash. The instant he saw us with the toddler he leapt up and began shouting, 'Oh no! No kids in here! You can't put them in my room. I'm smoking hash all the time!' Our other potential roommate began to berate us about the irresponsibility of travelling with a young child, which he admitted to considering a god. Mrs Calico cared for neither the smoking, the confession about the hash, nor the indignant protestations of the Japanese guest. We were admonished, all of us, that we would share this room till the next morning. None of us were happy. But none of us argued. We weren't quite game to go against her command. And anyway, she had given it and promptly departed.

FORTY-FOUR

Pigs Might... Eat Shit

EVERY COUNTRY HAS ITS OWN UNIQUE TOILET STORIES, but for diversity, India has it all covered. There are the Western ones that look as if they work, and then you discover, post deposit, that the damn thing doesn't flush. There are the Western ones that look as if they haven't worked since the British Raj installed them. There are the ceramic launch pads on the floor, where you hover over a hole and splash water over your arse when you're done. And sometimes there is just a curtained-off area in the middle of a field, with a Hessian flap door and no discernible designated place to go. I came across one of those high in the Himalaya with my two-year-old son in my arms. But that's another story.

There was even one I could not have imagined in my wildest dreams at the home of Dr Chen, a toothless Indian gentleman dressed only in a tiny red and white checked dhoti. Despite his misleading name, he was not a doctor, but an opportunist, who allowed random foreigners to share his hearth and sleep in the loft above his barn.

Dr Chen, clad in his dusty piece of cloth, greeted us warmly when we arrived in his small village. James had met him on a previous trip through India and stayed in his home. Whether he did or not, he made out that he remembered us, which led me to think otherwise, since I hadn't accompanied James on his previous trip.

After taking tea with the family and catching up on the four-year hiatus between visits, Dr Chen showed us to our 'room'. We had to climb a rickety wooden ladder to a room whose ceiling was rather too low for standing fully upright. But since we only intended to sit and sleep there, that seemed a small issue. I enquired after the bathroom, and Dr Chen indicated in the general direction of a small wooden shed. Because I was now used to quaint Indian toilet arrangements, I didn't think any more about it. Until the time came to make a deposit.

I entered the makeshift hut carefully, making sure there were clean spaces on which to place my feet. To my delight, the dirt floor had a short cement slipway stretching from the centre of the shed to an opening low in the back wall. There were squat pads at one end of the slide, down which the deposits obviously flowed, then passed out through the hole in the rear of the building. As I crouched down and prepared myself for the task, I noticed a long, sturdy stick standing in the corner, purpose unknown.

What happened next nearly launched me clear off the squat pads and through the thatched roof.

There was a piercing screeching and outrageously loud scuffling noises behind me, as if two or three humongous beasts were fighting over the spoils about to approach them from inside the hut. I leapt up and turned at the same time, twisting awkwardly mid-stream, to see what the hell was going on behind me. To my absolute horror, there were indeed three hungry snouts snuffling and biting at the back of the slide. Each one appeared capable of tearing down the wall and coming inside with me at any moment.

Immediately, I understood the purpose of the stick. Amazing how terror can have that effect on the learning curve. I grabbed it and started beating and flailing at the grotesque pink schnozzles. It had little effect, other than to make them angry and more determined to get inside.

I gave up any hope of completing the task I had come to perform, hurriedly dressed, and exited the hut, only pausing to regain composure once I was a safe distance away. Three malicious-looking mothers eyed me malevolently from their enclosure. Surely this was the origin of the phrase, 'I had the shit scared out of me.'

FORTY-FIVE

Trekking with Babus

YEARS AFTER OUR FIRST TRIP TO NEPAL, we returned yet again, this time with our two children, aged one and seven. At these tender ages, they had already been to more countries than most people visited in a lifetime. Everyone had imagined, wrongly, that children would tie us down, make us stable and respectable. We would finally have to grow up. Not so. We never even considered it. If they were right, we were going to find out for ourselves. And if we were right, we would be the living proof that you could do things differently. So, here we were again in the depths of Asia, planning a trek into the Everest region with both the kids.

Our bus left at the ungodly hour of 5:30 a.m. Even at that hour the Kathmandu City Bus Park brimmed with activity. Ancient contraptions vied for pole position near the gates, their roofs laden with tons of excess baggage and passengers huddled under tarpaulins. One by one they rose, Phoenix-like, from the huge puddles, belching smoke and diesel fumes. Young lads acting as conductors bellowed destinations across the park.

A bus suddenly lurched and died in the middle of a small lake. Unfortunately, it was our bus. We tiptoed through the mud trying to save precious new trekking boots from a sodden fate. When we were close enough, the conductor grabbed my pack and hurled it onto the roof. Then somehow, he squeezed the four of us in the back door, shouting at the impassive crowd to make room for the *babus* – babies. Nobody moved. Nobody could.

The bus lurched again and, miraculously, kept moving this time. We all swayed and teetered with the sudden motion and, surprisingly, no one fell out the back door, which didn't appear to close. We weren't even out the gates and I was ready to call it quits. Twelve bone-crunching hours later, we arrived in the mythical village of Jiri, road head for the trek into the Khumbu region of Nepal; the point of no return.

At 7:30 the next morning the four of us stood before the main street lodge where we had spent the night, drinking steaming sweet *chia*, and watching the early birds. Already they were 200 metres above us, climbing out of town. Our seven-year-old complained. He wasn't walking up there! Our one-year-old insisted she wasn't going in the carrier. She wanted to walk.

Our one backpack was barely visible under three down jackets that didn't fit inside. Several unemployed porters, left over from the morning rush, quickly sized up our situation and tried to sell us their services. Stoically, we resisted, a decision I regretted halfway up the first hill, and mentioned loudly and bitterly. But it was too late; the die was cast.

About a week into the trek, we approached Lamjura, a difficult pass at 3,000 metres. The ascent towards it and the descent from it were both long and strenuous sections of the trail. We found ourselves at a teashop, still one hour short of the pass, at about 5 p.m. It was freezing already. Light rain had fallen all afternoon.

Though we were offered space on the floor of a makeshift teahouse, the idea of spending the night in a damp and draughty bamboo hut did not appeal. Persuaded by the safety in numbers theory, we decided to press on to the lodge at the top of the pass with a group of rowdy young Sherpa traders. By the time we began our ascent, they were all hopelessly and happily drunk.

We reached the snow line just on dark. While rummaging through the pack, I dropped the flashlight. And it broke. Luckily, a full moon rose and reflected enough light off the snow to enable us to pick out a narrow trail of mud and ice. We walked in the moon shadows of a stunted alpine forest. Whoops and shrieks from the sozzled party ahead broke the gloom. But the icy puddles and stones made walking treacherous. The Sherpas laughed hysterically as, turn and turn again, they stumbled and fell. Behind me I could hear the voice of seven-year-old cheerfulness saying, 'Don't worry, Ma. We'll get there!'

Every bend in the trail raised my hopes for release from the torment, but for an eternity none came. Then a light appeared in the distant darkness. But the last 200 meters to the lodge were a quagmire of ankle-deep mud. We plunged ahead, glad to simply be somewhere, anywhere. We burst through the door, bringing an icy gust of wind into a room full of ruddy faces and the smell of pancakes. Everyone laughed, even us. It was 8 p.m.

Despite now being used to foreigners puffing and panting through their villages and homes, the Nepalis were still interested in talking. The trails cut across numerous ethnic groups, each with their own brand of hospitality. Tamang, Magar, Rai, Sherpa; someone would always share a *rakshi* and a thousand questions. They especially loved children, and their own extensive broods delighted in entertaining ours.

In Namche Bazaar, a Sherpa trading village at 3,500 metres, our hosts provided far more than just a roof over our heads. During the evening meal, Noa disappeared into the kitchen, a busy place of boiling water, bubbling oil and hot ovens. A steep, open staircase led from it to the family's rooms above and below. In a panic, I flew in from the dining room to find the grandmother of the family attending a wok full of hot oil and chips with my daughter strapped to her back. 'No problem,' she laughed. 'You eat, eat. I look everything.' And indeed, she did.

North of Namche, the high peaks became our constant walking companions. Everest, the Nuptse-Lhotse ridge and the stunning Ama Dablam soared into the distant blue. After passing Thangboche Monastery, the slopes were barren and unforgiving. It was a lonely place, and we felt like insignificant intruders. But the views just kept improving, until we walked right underneath the Ama Dablam massif.

Late in the afternoon under darkening skies, the village of Pheriche seemed a mirage. Set in a valley of grey rivers and boulders, the stone huts were uninviting. The warmth of the Sherpa woman who single-handedly ran the Trekkers' Lodge was a stark contrast to the forbidding landscape. We sat in her kitchen, inches from the stove, drinking mugs of steaming hot chocolate.

From a bank of old coffee tins, the really big ones, *Didi* mixed ingredients for an endless string of orders: boiled potatoes, Tibetan bread, noodle soup, Sherpa stew, rice and dal, pancakes, apple *momo* (dumplings), tea, coffee, *rakshi*. Conversation died as we all tried to fill the gaps and squeeze out the cold.

Outside the night was hellish, and in the morning, foul weather greeted us. Heavy, grey clouds obscured the peaks, and a gusting wind drove a light rain up the valley horizontally. A few hours' walk to the north, the trail suddenly climbed steeply onto the scree of the Khumbu glacier, a difficult task to negotiate in the thin air. We decided not to persevere, as much for our own sakes as the kids', descending instead to the relative luxury of the lodge at Thangboche Monastery. As we walked away from the desolation of Pheriche, I was disappointed, and felt I had failed somehow. But walking allowed plenty of time for free, wild thoughts, and on the way down, I realised I was wrong.

No matter that this time we hadn't reached Base Camp this time, or Kala Pattar, or some other famous feature on a map. In terms of the spirit of family and adventure, our trip had been a blazing success. We had walked for three weeks among mountains the local people referred to as having many faces but no sides (Ama Dablam), the Mother Goddess of the Earth (Everest), and where no bird dares fly.

FORTY-SIX

So Now I'm a People Smuggler?

ONE OF THE BEST THINGS ABOUT TRAVELLING with two young children was meeting the locals. In many other ways, it was a nightmare. And therein lies a whole other book. But they certainly opened doors that would otherwise have remained firmly shut had we just been 'regular' tourists.

The Asians, on the whole, loved children, especially our very blond, blue-eyed versions. Having them with us got us moved to the head of the lines at airports, seated more comfortably on flights, served more quickly in restaurants, and welcomed into people's homes to play with their own children. Because of that, they learnt the local languages much quicker than we did. More than once, while carrying Mani around Kathmandu, some young lads had spoken to him in Nepalese. And he had answered them.

One such family who attached themselves to ours were the Kumars. They were what could be considered middle class Nepalis. They owned a profitable restaurant business. They owned their own two-storey home. Their two younger children attended private school.

And their eldest son studied abroad. They aspired to westernisation, and embraced it at every opportunity.

We had met Mr Kumar in the Freak Street restaurant he owned and operated. Every morning for weeks, we had been there for our daily fix of porridge, yoghurt, and a rough approximation of toast with Vegemite. It made the rest of the day go better. The frequency of our visits eventually prompted Mr Kumar to speak to us on more than a superficial level, beyond 'What will you be having this morning?' He already knew the answer to that question, but he still asked it every day.

We told him of our plans to trek and get out and about in the Valley, and in turn, he recommended places he thought we should see. We came and went from Nepal, but we always returned to him and his restaurant. And he loved to hear of our antics and adventures. We became more than acquaintances; we were more like makeshift friends.

One day, he confided in us his plan to escape the poverty of Nepal and make some real money, exporting Nepali handicrafts to the world. Since we were living in Japan at the time, he had decided that we could help him get his foot in the door to that country.

He had gathered together a group of random and ramshackle men of varying ages, whom he wanted to employ in his fledgling export business. These five 'good men' were each expert in their fields. These ranged from Tibetan paintings, to woollen garments, to local handicrafts and more.

The first task set down for them was to accompany him to the next Tokyo International Trade Fair, to be held in the summer. His cunning plan was for us to 'interview' them, to ensure they were all up to speed on their specialities and would survive the Japanese immigration minefield on paper and in person.

Mr Kumar had told the men that he had contacted some bigwigs from Japan, and they had come to Nepal for the express purpose of testing his team's English skills and product knowledge in preparation for the trade fair. That was a joke. The only thing we knew about the products he intended to offer for export was that it was going to take a lot of them to fill the humongous double stall he planned to book in the Exhibition Hall. He would arrange the packing and shipping. We had just to receive the goods. Two hundred kilograms of them, as it turned out.

On the appointed day, at about 11 a.m., we arrived at Mr Kumar's home to meet his family and the proposed candidates. Mrs Kumar was a short rotund woman with heavy-framed spectacles that made her eyes look enormous. It was a bit frightening to first meet her; she seemed to be right in your face. But there was nothing judgemental about her. She was just the agreeable Nepalese wife of a reasonably well-off businessman and mother of his two polite and well-behaved children. After the ordeal that was the interviews, she served us up a plate of home-cooked *dal baht*, followed by the best rice pudding in the whole of Asia.

Mr Kumar had thought of everything, even the clothes he thought we should be wearing. At his insistence, we donned the garments he had prepared and were transformed into a Nepalese version of a foreign business tycoon and his wife, visiting from Japan. I ended up looking rather like Mr Kumar's wife, and with due respect to the woman, that wasn't particularly appealing. It was, however, quite a change from my usual getup of cuffed hippie pants, long flowing shirts and what I liked to call my 'mouse shoes,' a simple pair of black velvet Tibetan scuffs. My 'transformation' left me feeling uncomfortable and self-conscious.

The candidates were a poor picking, I must say. Of the five Mr Kumar had chosen, two were unavailable but did have passports, a definite plus considering the time frame we were working under. The first young man could neither understand nor speak a word of English. He smiled very nicely though, showing a perfect row of brilliant white teeth. The next gentleman knew absolutely nothing about anything on the shipping list and was desperately studying the craft of *tanka* painting, and English, in preparation for his interview. He'd had little success with either.

The last was an older man, probably well into his fifties. His English was hilarious but tolerable. Amazingly, he thought he was the next Oracle, and spoke at length about everything other than Nepalese handcrafts and foreign trade fairs. He had travelled widely in India, the only place most Nepalis could ever afford to go, and obviously considered himself worldly and wise. I nearly burst the seams on Mrs Kumar's *kurta* trying not to explode into hysterics, not so much at what he said, but the way that he said it. The whole time he spoke, his head moved in the typical Indian wobble. That completely did my head in.

When we returned to Japan, we became the victims of Mr Kumar's endless phone calls and parcel deliveries. Unfortunately, the Japanese Embassy in Kathmandu had routed one of his candidates, refusing to allow him to bring five people with him. I, for one, couldn't understand why he was so upset. Or so obviously desperate to get the last man his visa.

'Just bring the other four,' I commiserated. 'What's the drama?'

What I was blissfully unaware of at the time, was that Mr Kumar was charging each of his travel companions about $5,000 to accompany him to the fair to cover his costs. He needed the fifth man because he represented the profit factor. The first four were merely paying for the whole trip, products included.

Not long after their arrival, we visited them at their trade fair booth. It was not only huge, but a hopeless mess, as well. In a country where presentation and packaging were so highly-prized, their booth setup was not doing them any favours. We spent two days there, prior to the opening, arranging and rearranging the goods to the best of our untrained ability.

It was also during that time that we noticed he seemed to be short a couple of workers. Two of the interviewees were conspicuously absent. When we quizzed him on this, he motioned vaguely with his hand as if to dismiss them. Apparently, they had found better things to do with their time. 'No loss,' he pronounced. 'They're English was no good, anyway.'

Suddenly, the penny dropped. Not only was this whole enterprise a profit-making venture, dependent on the fifth man. It was also a one-way ticket. None of the participants had any intention of leaving the country at the completion of the trade fair. The missing workers had simply disappeared early. I couldn't quite believe that we had inadvertently become involved in his scheme. Or the lengths that he had gone to to pull it off. But at the same time, there was nothing we could do about it either.

And therein lay the caveat; beware of Greeks bearing gifts, lest you, too, become a people smuggler.

FORTY-SEVEN

Night Boat to Phangan

WE RETURNED TO KOH PHANGAN IN 1987, at the end of a long journey through India, Burma and Nepal. This time we took the night ferry direct from Suratthani. It left the mainland dock at 11 p.m., a two-deck ship with two deck classes. On the lower deck, passengers slept on the floor, unless they happened to have their own bedding. On the upper deck, where we were, we were provided with a paper-thin mattress. These were laid next to each other on either side of the deck with a walkway through the middle. As I rolled out my sleeping bag, I was intensely grateful for the layer that would separate me from the ghosts of travellers past, and their diseases and afflictions. It was a small blessing.

As the engines roared into life and we steamed our way out of the harbour, the Thai people travelling with us mostly laid down and tried to sleep. It was quite late, after all. But the *falang* either propped themselves up with a torch and a book, or chatted amongst themselves. A group of Germans decided it was time to get stoned, and three of them and their Thai lady friend stumbled over everyone else to get out to the open space at the stern of the boat.

When they returned to their berths amidships, they opened a bottle of *Mekong* whisky and proceeded to party. They seemed not to care too much that the rest of us were trying to have 'quiet time'. Nobody cared that they came and went periodically, until they returned without their Thai friend. Let's call her Mary, because I have no idea what her name was.

Mary returned to find the threesome seated on their allotted beds, swigging from a communal bottle of Mekong. Suddenly, she became upset. Very upset. She started yelling, and swearing, and accusing Gunther of flirting with the German woman, Sylvie. Full of Mekong, and high as a kite to boot, he argued back, vehemently and loudly.

Mary pleaded with Gunther to leave the others and go with her to the lower deck. Gunther replied by telling her she was crazy, and to calm down. It seemed that the problem was all in her head, as far as Gunther was concerned, anyway. Mary was having none of it, and all four of them became embroiled in a violent argument, which began to spill over onto the rest of the sleeping passengers. It started to get ugly. Everyone was awake now and intensely interested in the unfolding drama.

For a few short minutes, Mary disappeared. But amused interest from those around us turned to panic when Mary returned, wielding one of the empty *Mekong* bottles.

'I bring you come!' she screamed as she let fly in a wild swing. All arms went up to intercept her attack. Those closest to the action fled, and the foursome fell on each other in a melee of arms and legs.

Sylvie screamed for everyone to stop. Mary screamed insane, jealous words. Whisky and coke splashed in all directions. Gunther grabbed his flailing girlfriend, attempting to restrain her. But nothing placated her now.

Suddenly, a huge Italian tank of a man stood over the wrestlers, livid and totally out of control.

'Bastardos!' he boomed. 'Let her go!' mistaking the situation for an attack on the Thai woman.

Sylvie begged him, 'You don't understand. She makes the problem. Please take her, please!' He lunged towards Mary, presumably to rescue her, and Sylvie threw whisky in his face. The wrestling became full-blown fighting.

In desperation, Gunther grabbed Mary and began dragging her towards the open windows, obviously intending to throw her out. Sylvie was still pounding on Mary's head with her fists.

'Sleep! Sleep! Sleep!' A terrified Thai woman from across the aisle tried to intervene. 'If you make problem, tomorrow you stay with police. You want good holiday or not?'

'I kill the lady!' bellowed Gunther, too angry now to care about his vacation. 'Everything is ruined. Everything!'

Mary stopped fighting and dissolved into a fit of sobs. Another innocent bystander cradled and cajoled her until she agreed to accompany him to the other end of the boat. The three Germans disappeared downstairs again.

No one could sleep now, fearing another attack from the distraught Mary, perhaps another empty bottle on the wrong head. We all eyed each other warily, wondering how many other crazies may be lurking among our ranks.

'I feel like I'm in a movie, a bad one,' exclaimed the guy on the other side of me, shaking his head. None of us could quite believe what had just happened.

When the boat docked at Tongsala pier at 6 a.m. the next morning, Mary and Gunther lay together, sleeping like babies, their arms entwined.

And just like that, we had arrived back in paradise. The sheer number of *falang* that accompanied us on the overnight ferry should have alerted me to the shape of things to come, but it didn't. I was obsessed with the dream in my head, the memory of the beach, and the peace to which I was about to return.

FORTY-EIGHT

Haadrin Revisited

GOING BACK TO SOMEWHERE you've been before is often a mistake. Especially if that place occupies a special place in your heart, as Haadrin did mine. It had been three years, and I must confess that my expectations were high, and I should have known better than to think that nothing would have changed. Even the way we arrived should have been a clue that my special piece of paradise had been 'discovered'.

Instead of the motorbike taxi ferrying us along jungle paths to the tiny unworthy boat stranded in the shallows, we were loaded into a pick up with a canopy and narrow padded seats on either side of the tray. More people than could humanly fit accompanied us, most of them *falang*.

For a few kilometres, the road, although gravel, was smooth and dusty. But before long it became rough and rutted, and more suited to a four-wheel drive vehicle travelling at a much slower speed than the one we were in. The closer we got to the beach, the worse it got, until we were all trying to stand up and hang on to the canopy to avoid being uncontrollably bounced out of our seats by random boulders on the track. The last 100 metres of the road smoothed out again, and we travelled slowly into town past cafes, shops, banks, and travel agencies.

The narrow jungle path we had previously walked by torchlight had been transformed into a buzzing tourist spectacle. And the gentle peace and calm of Haadrin that I had fallen in love with was gone.

The first thing I noticed were the footprints in the sand. There was not one place on the beach unmarked by human traffic. The sounds of civilisation, in the form of every kind of music, emanated from an endless chain of restaurant and bungalow sets lining the beachfront and climbing the steep, rocky cliffs of the headlands at both ends. Our old friend's bungalows still occupied their prime position at the northern end of the beach. But when we sought them out, it was a sad reunion indeed.

We had arrived on the heels of the infamous full moon party, a night of music, dancing, drinking, sex, and drugs. Mr Chan's wife greeted us warmly, but when we gestured towards the beach with a questioning look, she lamented, 'Busy like this all the time. Last night full moon. All night noise, noise!'

Mr Chan explained that they only planned to stay one or two more years, then move on to a more peaceful part of the island, somewhere more like the old Haadrin that they left Bangkok to find. We wished them luck with that.

While progress marched on, and everything changed, I counted myself one of the lucky ones. I got to see Haadrin in all its glory. I got to stay there at a time when hardly anyone even knew the name of the pristine beach. It had become a place for young backpackers to retreat from the struggles of the Asian back roads and byways, to unwind into their own familiar versions of relaxation. Just like Koh Samui. This had brought its own baggage, not least of which was way too much rubbish and no way to get rid of it. The flotsam of society loitered on the water's edge, bobbing back and forth in the lapping wavelets.

Then there were the drugs. It was obvious they were everywhere. The full moon parties were just the tip of an ugly iceberg that had floated into the bay and decided to stay. It was difficult to tell who had been corrupted by whom - the *falang* or the Thais. The old chicken and the egg dilemma. The drugs were here so the people came. But the people who came also brought more demand for the drugs.

It just reinforced my conviction that going back was sometimes going to be the wrong decision.

FORTY-NINE

If a Tree Falls in the Forest

I wasn't a big fan of Malaysia. Until we visited the national park. We'd only ever passed through, going from Singapore to Thailand or vice versa. There was the mandatory stop in Penang to pick up a Thai visa, and to eat some of the best Indian food on the planet. But apart from that, it always seemed to be far too hot. I'm not sure that I should have expected anything less from a country so close to the equator.

In 1989, we were on a bit of a national park kick. Malaysia had several jungles worthy of note, not least of which was *Taman Negara*, two words that literally mean national park. It was located right in the centre of the Malay peninsula, easy enough to get to by public transport, but a world apart from anywhere we had ever been.

Access to the park headquarters was via a canopied long boat trip up river on a muddy brown, fast-flowing current. On either side, the jungle reached right down to the waterline. Now and then we passed large colourful birds sitting in the trees, and often heard the sound of the jungle creatures calling to each other to announce our passing.

The thing to do once we had been set up in the camping area was secure any food we had in the 'kitchen' - just a small shack with a thatched roof and walls of open mesh wire. Securing was a fairly loose term that involved wrapping everything even remotely edible in plastic and suspending it high above the benches on string lines.

Apparently, the jungle residents had become very adept at seeking out and destroying any unattended consumables.

The other thing to do there was walk. Numerous trails departed from HQ in several directions, all leading deeper into the jungle. We soon discovered that these trails, slushy and muddy from the frequent rainfall, were alive with leeches. And they were all busy standing on their tails ready to hook into our flesh as we passed above them.

Oh, the joy of removing heavy trekking boots to find your socks full of blood, leaking from an unseen source; then finding the fat, black, slug-like thing firmly attached to the sole of your foot. Ugh! Mani screamed. I nearly fainted. And it wasn't even on my foot! James was the first one to be assaulted in this way. For this reason, salt was a highly sought after commodity in these parts. Personally, I promptly invested in a one-pound bag of the stuff to add a little extra weight to my day pack, as if it weren't heavy enough already.

At the same time as we booked our night-in-the-jungle experience, we also bought two of the largest cans of insect and creepy crawly repellent we could find from the HQ shop. They were huge. I wasn't leaving any room for doubt.

We were going to be spending a night in an elevated jungle hide, two hours' boat ride further up river, and about a one-hour walk on a trail that ran perpendicular to the river, straight into the heart of the forest. Prior to our departure the next morning, I pulled my thickest pair of long socks up over the outside of my trousers and emptied the entire contents of the can of repellent over my legs, feet and boots. Overkill? No, just prepared for the worst.

We were dropped off on the riverbank at a makeshift dock consisting of a few planks of wood straddling some precarious upright logs. It was lucky we only had day packs on our backs, as the balancing act required to get out of the boat and onto the dock without making a splash was a delicate manoeuvre.

Four of us headed off in the same direction, and two more went off on a trail that followed the banks of the river. I remember thinking how brave they were. Anything could have been lurking in the shallow waters or the trees that hung low over the water. And probably was. I expected to soon hear screams, as they were torn limb from limb and devoured by wild animals.

The hide was built on high stilts with a steep open staircase leading to the viewing platform and sleeping area. Outward-opening shutters in the front wall provided a birds' eye view of a natural salt lick. Later in the evening, the natural watering hole would hopefully receive visits from various wild animals that lived in these parts of the thick jungle. We sat up practically all night, taking turns with our fellow hide-guests to keep vigil. We were as quiet as mice in the hide as we went about whatever tasks we could find to keep ourselves occupied by dim torchlight while we waited. But the noise outside in the inky black night was deafening.

We did get to see a couple of smaller animals - some wild boar mainly. But the thrill and highlight of the night was a young bull elephant that crashed through the undergrowth during the early hours of the morning. We had been able to hear him approaching for some time before he appeared. It sounded like he was ripping the jungle apart. He spent quite a while stomping around the open ground between us and the salt lick before wandering off to tear down a few banana palms. We came face to face with his handiwork the next morning, as well as his massive footprints on the muddy trail.

Zen masters are fond of asking questions, koans they call them, that put your mind into a spin, trying to logically resolve an impossible situation. They don't necessarily have rational answers. One of the most famous goes something like this: 'If a tree falls in the forest, does it make a sound if no one is there to hear it?' Well, I'm here to tell you that although there may not be anyone around to hear it, and whether or not it makes any noise, it still falls.

I know this because we spent many hours the day after our night in the hide, traipsing the hot, sweaty, dense, muddy, leech-ridden trail back to park HQ. We could have taken the easy way out and hopped another long tail back to camp, but no. No easy downstream floating under shady canopies for us. We had to do it the hard way - and the much more interesting and dangerous way. We had to trek through the jungle, chancing random attacks by big cats and wild elephants. Not to mention leeches and native Malayans with huge spears, still living traditional hunting and gathering lives under the dense canopy.

So, anyway, back to the trees that fall quietly? They mainly fall across jungle paths, so it seems. And they turn walking those paths into feats of strength and contortion that would make any decent rock climbing wall feel unworthy. Some of the smaller blockages had already been dealt with by previous passers-by, who were obviously carrying chainsaws with them for this very purpose. But the larger obstacles, the trees with a girth of at least two meters, posed less straightforward solutions - either find a way around them or start climbing. It was exhausting in the debilitating heat. We not only had to get ourselves and our packs from one side to the other, but Mani also had to be hauled up one side and then gently dropped down the other side. It was a bitter shame there were only two of us to manage it. A human chain of five or six would have got the job done much more quickly and efficiently. We all came away with more than a few scrapes and bruises for our efforts.

In the early afternoon, the trail led us almost through the middle of a native encampment. I think we were as surprised to see them as they were to see us, or more specifically, our five-year-old son. They probably saw many tourists pass this way, but I guessed that they probably hadn't seen too many young Caucasian children. They stopped what they were doing and silently followed us with their gaze until we were out of sight. It was intimidating, but not frightening. We just kind of observed each other in silence.

The Malaysian government has attempted to resettle these hunter-gatherer tribes into purpose-built accommodation on the outskirts of the national park. But the Batek people have resisted, favouring the shaded jungle canopy over huts in exposed clearings. And who could blame them?

It took the better part of eight hours to get back to camp, only to find the local monkeys had figured out a way to get into the kitchen shack and beaten us to our dinner. They left the scraps for an army of huge black ants that were intent on ferrying the spoils out of the kitchen and back to their tribes. Excellent. Exhausted. And now starving as well.

FIFTY

Seven Days on $100

THE WAY HOME TO JAPAN, following several weeks' trekking in Nepal and the jungles of Malaysia and Borneo, did not go smoothly. We had run out of cash. Before leaving Kathmandu, we had tried, unsuccessfully, to get our Japanese bank to respond to a request to wire some money from our bank account. Despite several tested telexes sent from a reputable bank in Kathmandu, there had been no reply. Desperately disappointed, we decided to try again from Hong Kong.

Unfortunately, we arrived in Hong Kong just prior to Easter. Another bank sent another round of requests, all of which were ignored, and then they all closed for the Easter break. We already had our tickets back to Tokyo via Taipei, so with just $100 USD to our names, we had no choice but to wing it. From studying the guidebooks, I knew that Taiwan was not the cheapest place on Earth. But I figured we could manage it if we were careful with our cash. Mani had to be the first priority, of course. I was only a little worried. We had been through worse.

On our arrival in Taipei, the prevailing exchange rate between US dollars and New Taiwanese dollars afforded us the princely sum of $1035 New Taiwanese dollars, which was going to have to last the three of us, two adults and a three-year-old, a whole week. It was a daunting challenge.

Back in the dark ages of airline ticketing, it was necessary to reconfirm booked flights to avoid your seat being reallocated to another ticket holder. Such an event would have meant total disaster for us at that point in time. That's why it was the first thing we did after collecting our luggage from the carousels. The clerk at the China Airlines counter was a pleasant young man, who more than happily reconfirmed our onward flights and put us down for vegetarian meals. Now all we had to do was survive the week on next to no money.

After setting aside the bus fares from the city back to the airport and the cash we needed for our departure tax, we were left with a daily budget of NT$100. We managed to find a decent enough room in the city for NT$15 per night. It wasn't luxurious, but it was clean and warm. We figured out that if we fed Mani breakfast and lunch as a top priority, we could afford for all of us to eat dinner and still have a little spare cash for some sightseeing around the city. Luckily for us, there was a cheap and delicious vegetarian cafe just down the road from our hostel. We ate there every evening for the entire week.

Our sightseeing was limited to places that were free, like the museums, and the beautiful Chinese gardens dotted around the city. We fed ducks in the parks, and walked miles and miles to find examples of outstanding Chinese architecture. It was the worst thing we could have done, because it made us even hungrier. But it saved us from spending every waking moment in our hostel room dreaming of the next meal.

The vegetarian cafe turned out to be much cheaper than we had budgeted for, and with the savings we made, we managed to make a day trip out of the city to the east coast and Taroko Gorge. The weather was rainy and crap, but we all enjoyed the change of scenery and diet, even if it was for just one day and night.

I had never felt quite as alone as I did during that week in Taipei. There was no fall back, no one to help out. I was bitterly disappointed and angry with our Japanese bank, and closed the account with them the minute we returned. They didn't care. They bowed profusely as we left the building, having caused quite a scene, as only foreigners can. But beyond that I was just another crazy *gaijin* (foreigner). But no one knew of our predicament in the moment. No one understood what we had to deal with. There wasn't even anyone I could complain to. It wasn't fair. We had loads of cash that we couldn't access. It wasn't our fault. But I just had to find the strength to endure it, to put up and shut up.

Finally, the day came for us to fly back to Tokyo. My budgeting skills had gotten us through the week, and we made it back to the airport with exactly NT$7 left in my pocket. We had had to skip dinner the night before, and breakfast earlier that morning, so we were desperately looking forward to our inflight vegetarian lunches. Everything was going to be okay. As soon as we arrived in Tokyo, we would hit up the nearest ATM and catch the train home and eat more food than we had for the whole of the week just gone.

I handed our tickets over at the China Airlines check in counter and waited expectantly to be handed our boarding passes. The young lady smiled at me sweetly, then said the only words I didn't want to hear. 'I'm sorry, but your tickets have been cancelled.'

'What!' It was unbelievable. Literally. I opened my mouth to ask why, but no words came out.

'You did not reconfirm your flight,' she went on.

I think at that point I needed to sit down, but instead I engaged the warp drive. I spoke so quickly, and at such a high pitch, that the poor girl had a great deal of trouble understanding me. I babbled hysterically about how we had reconfirmed on our arrival, how we had survived an entire week on just $700 NT dollars, how we had gone hungry so that our son could eat, how we had seen so little of

Taiwan because of the Japanese bank not sending us any of OUR OWN money, and how I now had just $7 NT dollars left in my pocket and couldn't even afford to leave the airport again. I slammed the few remaining coins down on the counter to prove the depths of our poverty. But she was unmoved.

The best she could offer was standby. We might get on the plane, we might not. We would just have to wait. As if it might make a difference, she suggested that we should try to find the young man who had (not) reconfirmed our tickets a week ago. Right! Find one Chinese man, whose face I neglected to memorise a week ago, in an airport full of Chinese men. As stupid as that idea was, I did try it. But he was nowhere that I could find him.

At the eleventh hour, as the gate for our flight was closing, we were summoned back to the check in counter. Good news. Someone had not turned up. We could get on the plane. The bad news - there would be no vegetarian meals available at this late stage of boarding. I think my shoulders must have visibly sagged at the news.

'You will have to hurry,' she continued, still unemotional and unmoved by our plight.

We made it to the gate with seconds to spare. The young man at the door to the air bridge asked for our boarding passes. As I handed them to him, I looked up into his face. Shock! Horror! There he was! Unmistakably. It was him.

'You!' I shouted at him. Instantly, his smile turned to fear. I knew he knew who I was. I knew he knew what he had (or rather hadn't) done. I wanted to tear him limb from limb and set him on fire. But the plane was about to leave. And with or without a meal between here and Japan, we were going to be on it.

'Have a nice flight,' I heard him say to the back of my head as I disappeared down the corridor.

So cruel.

Epilogue

'The difference between being a tourist and a traveller is that a traveller is open to unplanned experience and doesn't have her nose stuck in a guidebook, tracking down famous sites. She ventures out from behind glass windows (in hotels and touring buses) and meets people. She connects.'

From *Life is a Trip* (2012) by Judith Fein

The story doesn't end there. A big piece of it is missing from this book, the part where we moved to Japan with a nine-month-old and just two backpacks between the three of us. It's a story of great risk and even greater reward, the trouble you can get into when choosing to fly by the seat of your pants, and the fun you have trying to get out of that trouble.

Though we originally planned to stay in Japan only long enough to make some money to continue our travels, we ended up living in our little house in the middle of the market gardens just outside Tokyo for over eight years. The more we stayed, the more we couldn't tear ourselves away, though we took many extended breaks to visit other Asian countries. It was a common experience for many of the expats we met there. The only difference was that we had children, two by the time we left.

Moving to another country with a baby and no job to go to was far from a normal, or rational, thing to do. But then, when did we ever do anything that was expected of us? It was eight years of close encounters with the Japanese people, their kindness and generosity, their devotion to duty, ritual and obligation, and the hilarious misunderstandings that happen when East meets West.

Keep an eye out on Amazon for the sequel to Restless

Gaijin Live Next Door

I want to thank you for purchasing my book. I hope you have enjoyed reading it as much as I enjoyed writing it. And living it.

I'd also really appreciate you **leaving an honest review** on the Amazon.com website.

Please also feel free to email me your thoughts and comments at

heather@heatherjhackett.com

Namaste

Heather Hackett

About the Author

Heather Hackett is not just an author. She is also a poet, a traveller, a photographer, a musician, a free spirit, an adventurer, a thrill seeker, a gym junkie, a cycling nut, a wife and a mother. She wears all these hats with confidence and style and brings her entire self to everything she does.

She has cycled across entire countries, camped under freeways, trekked the Himalaya with a baby on her back, lived in a bamboo hut on a Thai beach, worked as a cleaner in a motel, taught English to the Japanese, and been executive assistant to a Deputy Prime Minister of Australia. There's nothing she can't do or won't try – at least twice. If she doesn't know, she makes it her mission to find out.

Heather currently lives in Newcastle, Australia with her partner, Iain, and best furry friend, Lea.